COMPUTER PROGRAMMING
IN PASCAL

David Lightfoot first learnt Pascal while studying computing at the University of Essex. After graduating, he worked as a commercial programmer and then as a lecturer before becoming principal lecturer at ICL Training, where he developed and taught courses on Pascal, COBOL and FORTRAN. He now teaches structured programming and computer graphics at Slough College of Higher Education.

D1390081

TEACH YOURSELF BOOKS

COMPUTER PROGRAMMING IN PASCAL

David Lightfoot

TEACH YOURSELF BOOKS
Hodder and Stoughton

First published 1983
Third impression (with amendments) 1986
Sixth impression 1990

Copyright © 1983
David Lightfoot

British Library Cataloguing in Publication Data

Lightfoot, David
    Computer programming in Pascal.——(Teach yourself)
    1. PASCAL (computer program language)
    I. Title
    001.64′24   QA76.73.P2

ISBN 0 340 33728 1

Printed and bound in Great Britain for
Hodder and Stoughton Educational,
a division of Hodder and Stoughton Ltd,
Mill Road, Dunton Green, Sevenoaks, Kent,
by Richard Clay Ltd, Bungay, Suffolk
Phototypeset by Wyvern Typesetting Ltd, Bristol

Contents

Introduction

Pascal is a modern, high-level programming language whose chief advantage lies in its structure. This presents itself in two ways: Firstly, the statements that constitute the action of a program can be combined in a natural, structured way, which means that programs are easy to write and read. Secondly, the data that a program uses is itself capable of being structured in powerful and flexible ways which also lead to its natural and clear use in programs. In this way the structure of Pascal leads to clarity in programs, which is the most important aid to writing programs that are reliable and easy to maintain.

Although Pascal offers very powerful and flexible facilities, its designers were aware of the costs, in terms of space and speed, of advanced facilities in a language and so they compromised carefully. This has resulted in a language that is both powerful and very efficient in terms of the time and space required to run programs written in it.

Pascal's academic origins led it to be regarded for some time as an academic's language, but in the last few years its usefulness in all areas of programming has been realised, largely due to the wide availability of microcomputers.

The language is now available on a variety of machines ranging from very large mainframes to microcomputers and differences in implementations of the language are usually so small that programs written for one machine can be transported easily to another of a different make.

A further point of interest is that Pascal is the language which forms the basis of the US Department of Defense's Higher Order Language, Ada, which seems likely to become an important programming language of the future. Ada is a large, complex language, which is probably best approached through Pascal as an intermediary.

Origins

The name 'Pascal' does not stand for anything. The language is named after the famous French mathematician and philosopher Blaise Pascal (1623–1662), who invented a mechanical calculator to help his father, a tax collector, do calculations.

The language was devised in 1970 by Professor Doctor Niklaus Wirth (pronounced 'Veert'), who is head of the Computer Science Department at the Swiss Federal Institute of Technology (Eidgenössische Technische Hochschule – ETH) in Zurich, Switzerland.

Wirth was involved in various developments of an earlier high-level language, Algol 60 (such as Euler and Algol W). He later turned his attention to the teaching of programming and found that no existing language embodied the structured programming concepts devised by himself and others, such as Professors Dijkstra and Hoare.

Pascal owes much to Algol 60 in its design and will initially seem familiar to those who know that language, but it contains further facilities for the structuring of instructions and, especially, for the structure of data.

High-level languages

High-level languages are those that attempt to provide facilities to fit the needs of the problem being solved by computer rather than fitting the binary code of a particular computer. Thus a high-level language is easier for the ordinary user who does not wish to be concerned with the intricacies of a computer. The only difficulty of using a high-level language is that computers do not understand them directly.

Programs must be either interpreted or compiled. Interpretation involves another program, an interpreter, looking at each line of the high-level language program, working out what it means and then performing the necessary action. Programs in the BASIC language are nearly always interpreted.

Compilation involves the program being translated, in its entirety, into the (binary) machine code of the computer. This is done by a program called a compiler, which also gives messages concerning errors in the syntax of the program.

P-code systems

Some implementations of Pascal involve both interpretation and compilation. The Pascal is compiled to produce P-code (Pascal code), which is a sort of artificial machine code (Fig. 1). To use Pascal on any given machine it remains only to write an interpreter for P-code. (The compiler itself can be written in Pascal.) This method gives great portability and has enabled Pascal to be implemented on a large number of machines in a short time.

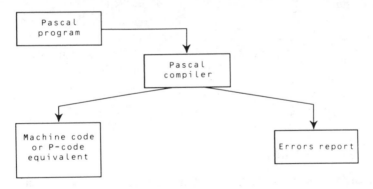

Fig. 1

The best known such implementation of Pascal is that produced by the University of California at San Diego (UCSD)* and which is available on a wide range of microcomputers. Although this implementation involves many non-standard features in the language, it is referred to frequently in this book because of its great popularity.

* UCSD Pascal is a trademark of the Regents of the University of California.

1

General Rules of Pascal

Layout rules

Pascal does not require statements to be written in special positions on the line. This means that it is quite acceptable to the compiler if you start all statements at the beginning of the line.

However, in order to make the program easier to read and understand, it is a good idea to indent statements – that is, to start them a certain distance in from the left to show the structure of the program. All the programs in this book have been laid out in this way.

Pascal words are separated from each other by one or more spaces (blanks), or a special symbol or by the end of a line.

Rules for identifiers

In order to identify the values that your program will work on, you will need to give them names. These are called identifiers.

1 Identifiers must be made up of letters and/or digits but they must begin with a letter. For example: `x, average, count`. Check with the Pascal manual for the implementation that you are using to see if it permits lower-case letters in identifiers.
2 Identifiers may not have spaces in them.
3 There is a restriction on the length of identifiers. The Pascal Report states that it should be the length of a line but most compilers impose (reasonably) a lower limit, typically of about thirty characters.

4 Additionally, the Pascal Report permits compilers to regard only the first eight characters of an identifier as significant. It is safest to assume that the compiler you are using takes advantage of this and to avoid using identifiers such as, for example, `temperate` and `temperature` in the same program.

Reserved words

Pascal has a small number of reserved words (35), such as `IF`, `PROGRAM`, `AND`, `WHILE`, which have special meanings and therefore are not available to you as identifiers. A list of these appears in Appendix A. You will find that you very quickly learn the reserved words when you start to use them in programs.

For ease of recognition, in this book reserved words are printed in capitals.

Standard words

There is a second group of special words that are standard or predefined. Although these can be used by you as identifiers, this will destroy their special meanings and so it is very unlikely that you will wish to do this. A list of these appears in Appendix B.

Meaningful identifiers

When you make up identifiers it is a good idea to take advantage of the fact that they can be fairly long even though this involves more writing and typing. A longer identifier can have more meaning for you and it is less likely that you will get confused about what it refers to. For example: use `chequecount` and `totalamount` rather than `c` and `t`.

The syntax diagrams

The rules for constructing statements in any language are called its syntax (or grammar).

The syntax of Pascal is usually expressed by means of syntax diagrams. These are very easy to understand – you just follow the arrows. Words in upper-case and punctuation symbols stand for themselves. Words in lower-case refer to other components of the syntax diagrams.

Since you already know some syntax (the syntax of an identifier), it should be easy for you to follow the syntax diagram shown in Fig. 1.1. All the syntax of Pascal is expressed in this form and it is collected in Appendix C.

Identifier

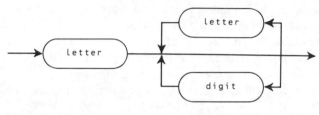

Fig. 1.1

Comments

Commentary information may be introduced anywhere where a separator could appear. Comments begin with the { (left-brace) symbol and finish with the } (right-brace) symbol.

What you put between these symbols will not be read by the computer but will remain visible in your program when you look at it. Since many computers do not have brace characters (* can be used for left-brace and *) can be used for right-brace. Do not put a space between (and * or * and).

Use comments to tell the reader of your program what it does and especially to explain any parts that are not self-evident.

Comments are particularly useful if you return to a program to modify it after some time. It is surprising how quickly you forget your own programs.

Exercises

1.1 State which of the following are both permissible and advisable as identifiers. For those which are not, say why:

(*a*) a
(*b*) datafile1
(*c*) xrolp5z
(*d*) xi/9
(*e*) passmark
(*f*) VAR
(*g*) code number
(*h*) real
(*i*) datafile2
(*j*) 7—up

2

The Standard Types
and their Use

The standard types

When writing a computer program you will want to represent the
sorts of values that exist on the real world, such as names, dates,
numeric quantities and so on. Pascal allows you to define your own
types to represent such quantities and these will be covered in
Chapter 5. However, Pascal provides four standard types:

Integer whole number: for example, age in years

Real   number with decimal point: for example, a tempera-
        ture in degrees Centigrade

Char   a character a to z, 0 to 9, punctuation, and so on

Boolean true or false, a logical value

Constants

Constant values may be of any of the four types or of type string
(PACKED ARRAY [1..n] OF char – see Chapter 7) as shown in
Fig. 2.1. Examples:

Integer constants: 27 -27 4 3259

Real   constants: 2.7 -27.0 4.0 0.3259 4.7E-6
        (E means 'times 10 to the power of')

Char   constants: 'A' 'Z' '?'. The apostrophe character is
        represented by writing it twice ''''

Boolean constants: False True

String constants: 'ABC' 'Pascal''s triangle'

Unsigned integer

Integer constant

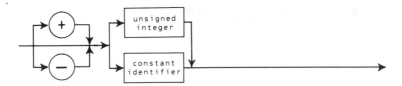

Real constant

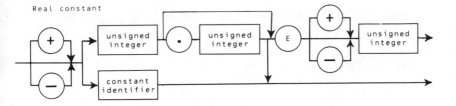

Boolean constant

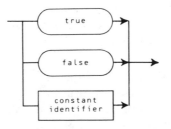

Character constant

Constant of type PACKED ARRAY [1 .. n] OF CHAR

Fig. 2.1

Declarations

You have already seen the rules for constructing identifiers. Identifiers can be used as names of areas for storing values. There are two sorts of values:

1 Some values that we give names to are unchanging. For example, in discussing the properties of circles the value of π (pi) is always 3.14159 (approx).
2 Other values can change while the program is running or from one use of the program to the next.

Declarations of named-constants

Values of the first sort are named-constants. You indicate your intention to use them by a declaration as shown in Fig. 2.2. For example:

```
CONST pi = 3.14159;
```

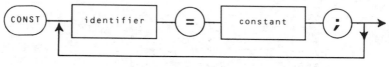

Fig. 2.2

Here, the identifier, pi, is given the constant value 3.14159, which the compiler deduces from its form to be of type real.

Hereafter, in the program, when the name pi is stated the compiler will replace it by 3.14159. This facility costs nothing in terms of the time and space taken by the program and adds to the ease of reading and altering the program. It also adds to the safety of a program, since you cannot accidentally change the value of such a constant.

Declarations of variables

Values of the second sort are called variables and are declared as shown in Fig. 2.3. For example:

```
VAR temp : real;
```

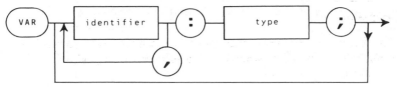

Fig. 2.3

Here the variable `temp` is given the type `real` but no value is given to it at this point, which means that at this stage its contents are undefined (and unpredictable).

Using both CONST and VAR

```
CONST pi = 3.14159;
VAR radius, area : real;
```

Note that : is used when declaring the type associated with an identifier, = for a value. Each declaration finishes with a semi-colon.

Examples of declarations of constants and variables

```
CONST    pi = 3.14159; (* type real *)
         zero = 0; (* type integer *)
         vrai = true; (* type boolean *)
         space = ' '; (* type char *)
         heading = 'Pascal program';
         (* type PACKED ARRAY [1..n] OF char (see
                                          Chapter 7) *)
VAR      radius : real;
         count : integer;
         firsttime : boolean;
         letter : char;
         (* variables of type PACKED ARRAY OF char are
         covered in Chapter 7 *)
```

Assigning values to variables

Values are given to variables by means of the assignment statement.

The expression can be simply a constant of the same type as the variable:

```
CONST fixed = 3;
VAR m, n : integer;

m:= 3;
n:=fixed;
```

or the name of another variable that already has a value:

```
n:= m;
```

or it may be a full integer, real or boolean expression. Semi-colons are used to *separate* statements.

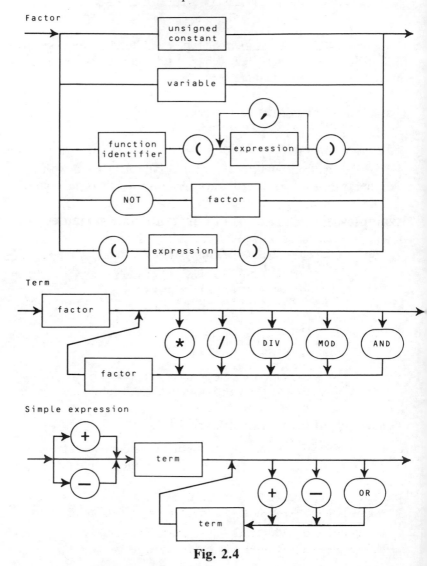

Fig. 2.4

Expression

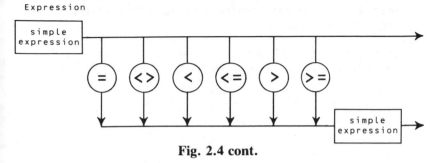

Fig. 2.4 cont.

Integer and real expressions

To make expressions involving integer or real values you can use the following operators:

+	addition
−	subtraction
*	multiplication
/	real division, for example: 19/4 is 4.75
DIV	integer division, for example: 19 DIV 4 is 4 (effect on negative values determined by implementation)
MOD	modulo value (remainder), for example: 19 MOD 4 is 3 a MOD b = a − (a DIV b)* b (effect on negative values determined by implementation)

DIV and MOD may only be used on integer values.

Values of type integer will automatically be converted to type real where necessary. For example:

```
VAR a : real;
    b : integer;

a := 0; (* a gets 0.0 *)
a := b;
```

but real values are never converted to integer since this would lose information. You must use the conversion functions:

```
b:=trunc (a) (truncate - lose fractional part)
b:=round (a) (round - to nearest integer)
```

where b is an `integer` variable and a is a `real` variable or
expression. For example:

```
b:=trunc (3.7) gives b the value 3
b:=trunc (-3.7) gives b the value −3

b:=round (2.4) gives b the value 2
b:=round (2.7) gives b the value 3
b:=round (−2.7) gives b the value −3
B:=round (2.5) gives b the value 3
b:=round (−2.5) gives b the value −3
```

Precedence of operators

The operators *, /, DIV, MOD have higher precedence than +, −
(applied to two operands). This means that multiplication, division
and modulus calculations are performed before addition or
subtraction. Thus:

```
a + b * c is equivalent to a + (b*c)
```

and

```
b/a−b means (b/a)−b
```

The precedence can be over-ridden by the use of brackets. For
example:

```
(a+b)*c
a/(2*b)
```

Within a level of precedence, evaluation is left to right so:

```
a/2*b means (a/2)*b
```

This can be changed by writing:

```
a/(2*b)
```

Exponential operator

Pascal has no operator for raising values to powers (↑ in BASIC, **
in FORTRAN). This is for reasons of efficiency, since this
operation is very costly in computer time. To help you, however,

there is a function called `sqr`, which gives the square of its `integer` or `real` parameter. For example:

```
y:=sqr (x) assigns x squared to y
p:=sqr (a*b+c)
```

If you really need to raise a value to a power you can use the standard functions `ln` and `exp`. (`x^y` is given by `exp ( ln (x) * y)` – see next section.)

Standard functions

Pascal provides several standard functions:

`sqr` and `abs` each return values of type `real` or `integer` depending on the type of parameter (argument) given in brackets.

```
sqr(i) gives i squared
sqr(3) gives 9
sqr (2.5) gives 6.25
abs(x) gives x if x>=0 otherwise −x
abs(−3) is 3
abs(3) is 3
abs(−27.52) is 27.52
```

Further functions that take `real` parameters and return `real` values are:

`sqrt(r)`	square root
`sin(r)`	sine of r (r in radians)
`cos(r)`	cosine of r (r in radians)
`arctan(x)`	arctangent of x (result in radians) (`atan` in UCSD Pascal)
`exp(x)`	exponential x
`ln(x)`	natural logarithm of x

2π radians = 360 degrees
1 degree = 0.0174532925 radians

Boolean **expressions**

`Boolean` expressions yield either `true` or `false` and can be built by applying relational operators to expressions.

The relational operators are:

```
>    greater  than
>=   greater  than  or  equal  to
=    equal  to
<>   not  equal  to
<    less  than
<=   less  than  or  equal  to
```

For example:

```
(a+b) < (c+d)
```
yields `true` if a + b is less than c + d,
otherwise it yields `false`.

Such a value can be assigned to a variable declared to be of type
`boolean` or can be used in branching or looping constructs
(Chapter 3). Note that brackets are needed around the arithmetic
expressions. This is because relational operators can also be applied
to values or expressions of type `boolean`. For example:

```
VAR       a,b,c,d : real;
          firstinorder,
          secondinorder,
          firstsameassecond : boolean;

firstinorder:=a < b;
secondinorder:=c < d;
firstsameassecond:= firstinorder = secondinorder;
```

Comparison of `real` **values**

`real` values cannot be represented with complete accuracy in a
computer. This means that all `real` values are necessarily
approximate. It is therefore unwise to test two `real` values for
equality (or inequality). Instead always test that `real` values differ
by less than a given tolerance value (determined by the application). For example:

```
CONST     tolerance = 1.0e-3;
VAR       a,b : real;
          same : boolean;

same := abs (a-b)<tolerance
```

Boolean **operators**

There are three operators that can be used for combining `boolean` expressions. These are:

```
NOT
AND
OR
```

Their precedence is such that `NOT` has greatest precedence, then `AND`, then `OR`. For example: `NOT a AND b OR c AND NOT d` where a, b, c and d are `boolean` variables is interpreted as if bracketed as follows:

```
((NOT a) AND b) OR (c AND (NOT d))
```

Note in particular that to negate an entire `boolean` expression it will be necessary to use brackets. For example:

```
l:=(a > b) AND firsttime
```

To give `l true` when the above expression gives `false` and vice versa, it will be necessary to write:

```
l:= NOT ((a > b) AND firsttime)
```

It is not correct to write:

```
l:= NOT (a > b) AND firsttime
```

De Morgan's rules

Two important rules of boolean algebra are due to Augustus de Morgan and, expressed in Pascal, are:

```
NOT (a OR b) is equivalent to NOT a AND NOT b
```

and:

```
NOT (a AND b) is equivalent to NOT a OR NOT b
```

The odd **function**

There is a standard function `odd`, which returns a `boolean` value when applied to an `integer` expression:

```
odd (integer expression)
```

The result is true if the `integer` expression is an odd number, otherwise it is false:

```
odd (1) is true
odd (256) is false
```

Character comparisons

There are no character operators in Pascal but characters can be used in `boolean` expressions. For example:

```
VAR b : boolean;
ch1,ch2: char;

b := ch1 = 'a'
```

yields `true` if `ch1` holds the character `'a'`, also:

```
b := ch1 = ch2
```

yields `true` if `ch1` holds the same character as `ch2`.

It is also possible to test character values using `<`, `<=`, `>`, `>=`, `<>`. This uses the underlying collating sequence (character code) of the machine you are using.

On most machines the characters 'A' to 'Z' (and 'a' to 'z') occupy adjacent values. Thus it is possible to test if a character is (upper-case) alphabetic by:

```
VAR ch : char;
    alpha : boolean;

alpha := (ch >='A') AND (ch <= 'Z')
```

However, certain character codes, notably Extended Binary Coded Decimal Interchange Code (EBCDIC) (but not American Standard Code for Information Interchange, ASCII), have a disjoint representation where the codes for 'A' to 'I' are an uninterrupted sequence, as are those for 'J' to 'R' and 'S' to 'Z'. However, other characters appear between 'I' and 'J' and 'R' and 'S'. The alphabetic test must then become:

```
alpha:= (ch >='A') AND (ch <='I')
    OR (ch >='J') AND (ch <='R')
    OR (ch >='S') AND (ch <='Z')
```

For the remainder of this book it will be assumed that the machine you will be using has an unbroken 'A' to 'Z'. You may need to make alterations to examples if your machine does not have this property. The same consideration applies to lower-case letters in the EBCDIC code.

The ord function

The ord function yields the ordinal (position) value of an expression within the list of all the values of a type:

```
ord (integer)    gives the integer itself.
ord (boolean)    gives 0 if false,
                 else 1 if true.
ord (char)       gives the numeric code value of the char-
                 acter, starting from zero (dependent upon
                 implementation).
ord (real)       not applicable (illegal).
```

There is an inverse to ord for type char:

```
chr (integer) gives the character with code value of the
integer.
```

For example, to convert a (numeric) character to the numeric (integer) value it represents:

```
int:= ord (ch) — ord ('0')
```

Note: in general ord ('0') is not zero.

To reverse the process:

```
ch:= chr (ord('0')+int)
```

To find the character 5 later than ch in the character code:

```
chplus5:= chr (ord(ch)+5)
```

Note: Beware of gaps in the character code.

Exercises

2.1 Write Pascal declarations for variables that are suitable for holding data of the following types:

(*a*) An examination mark (whole number).

(*b*) The average (mean) of several exam marks.

(*c*) A code – 'A' or 'O' indicating the level of the exam.

(*d*) Whether or not the candidate has passed the exam.
Write Pascal assignment statements to give the following
values to the variables declared above:

(*a*) 51

(*b*) 47.5

(*c*) A level

(*d*) Pass

2.2   Given the declarations:

```
VAR year : integer;
    leap : boolean;
```

Write Pascal statements to assign true to leap if year is a
leap year and false if it is not. A year is a leap year if it is
divisible by four (but not by one hundred) or divisible by four
hundred.

2.3   A grid reference consists of an eight-digit whole number of
which the left-most four digits give the 'eastings' (offset in an
easterly direction) and the right-most four digits give the
'northings'.

Write Pascal declarations and statements that assume the
values of two grid references and calculate the shortest
distance between them.

2.4   A moving body suffers an apparent contraction due to its
velocity relative to the observer (the FitzGerald contraction).
This is given by the relationship:

$$\text{length at speed} = \text{length at rest} \times \sqrt{1 - \frac{V^2}{C^2}}$$

where V is the velocity of the body in metres per second and C
is the velocity of light (299 792 458 metres/second).

Write Pascal declarations for the variables involved in this
relationship and, assuming that values for the length at rest
and the velocity of the body have been given, write Pascal
statements to assign the corresponding value to length at
speed.

2.5   A radar station detects enemy aircraft approaching. The radar
set gives an angle of elevation and a range in the direction of
the radar beam.

Write Pascal declarations and statements to calculate the altitude and horizontal range of the aircraft given the elevation in degrees and the range in arbitrary units. (*Note:* 1 degree = 0.0174532925 radians.)

3

Branching and Looping

Compound statements

Pascal allows great flexibility in the construction of programs and this is largely due to the concept of a compound statement.

A compound statement is a sequence of simple statements preceded by the reserved word BEGIN, followed by the reserved word END and separated from each other by semi-colons (Fig. 3.1).

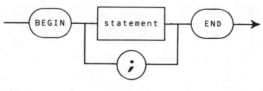

Fig. 3.1

For example:

```
BEGIN
    temp:=a;
    a:=b;
    b:=temp
END
```

can be regarded as a single (compound) statement. Note that there is no need for a semi-colon before an END since the semi-colon *separates* statements within a compound statement rather than terminating them. (The semi-colon *terminates* declarations).

If you do write a semi-colon before an END the compiler will assume that there is a null statement between the semi-colon and the END. You may prefer to put a semi-colon before an END to make it easier if you want to add another statement before the END at a later time.

The overall structure of a Pascal program

The program which follows uses the facilities introduced so far (and some output and input facilities). It is intended to work on any implementation of Pascal.

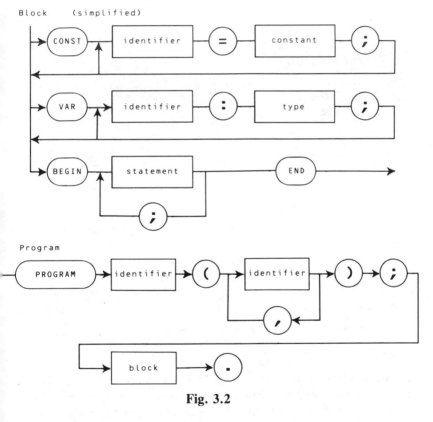

Fig. 3.2

If possible, try typing in and running this program on a computer with a Pascal compiler. When the program runs it expects as input from the keyboard (or card-deck) a real number that will be interpreted as a temperature in Fahrenheit. The program will print the equivalent temperature in Centigrade.

```
PROGRAM temperature (input, output);
(* example program called 'temperature'
uses some input and output statements which will be
covered in Chapter 4 *)
(* declarations *)

CONST ratio  =1.8;              (* constants *)
      offset =32;
      equiv  ='is equivalent to';
VAR   cent,
      fahr  : real;             (* variables *)

(* compound statement *)

BEGIN
   read ( fahr );    (* obtain fahrenheit
                        temperature from input *)
   cent := ( fahr — offset ) / ratio;
   writeln ( fahr : 5 : 2,' degs f' );
   writeln ( equiv );
   writeln ( cent : 5 : 2' degs c' )
END.
```

Note: Your system may restrict you to using upper-case letters.

Branching – the IF statement

Very often in a program it will be necessary for the action taken to depend on prevailing conditions, that is, the value of one or more of the variables of the program.

The most useful statement for branching is the IF statement (Fig. 3.3). In each case, the expression is a boolean expression. The statement can, of course, be a compound statement. For example:

```
VAR mark, passmark : integer;
    male : boolean;

IF mark >= passmark
   THEN passes := passes + 1;

IF male THEN retiringage := 65
        ELSE retiringage := 60;
```

The statement in the form of an IF statement can itself be an IF statement. This is known as nesting and can be repeated to any depth.

An ambiguity arises when an IF statement with an ELSE part is nested with one that has no ELSE part:

IF expression 1 THEN IF expression 2 THEN statement 1 ELSE statement 2

since it is not clear to which IF the sole ELSE part belongs. This ambiguity is resolved by a rule:

An ELSE part always belongs to the most recent unpaired IF.

Note that:

```
IF male
    THEN
      IF AGE > 65
         THEN
             retiredmen:=retiredmen + 1
    ELSE
        ladies:=ladies + 1
```

will not be interpreted as it looks since the ELSE will pair with IF age > 65. To achieve the effect indicated by the layout write:

```
IF male
    THEN
     BEGIN
        IF age > 65
          THEN
              retiredmen:=retiredmen + 1
      END
    ELSE
        ladies:=ladies + 1
```

(It is always incorrect to write a semi-colon before ELSE.)

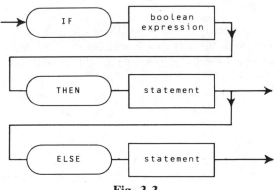

Fig. 3.3

Looping – the WHILE statement

Frequently in programming it is necessary to repeat a series of statements while a condition holds. This is easily written in Pascal by means of the WHILE statement, which has the format shown in Fig. 3.4, where the expression is a boolean expression and the statement may be a compound statement.

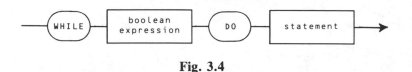

Fig. 3.4

Looping – the REPEAT statement

An alternative to the WHILE statement is the REPEAT statement, which has the form shown in Fig. 3.5.

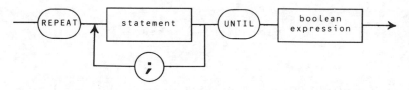

Fig. 3.5

The difference between the REPEAT statement and the WHILE statement is that in the REPEAT statement the test that terminates the loop is made *after* the statements have been carried out; in the WHILE statement the test is made *before*. The REPEAT statement is used when it is not possible to make the test until the statements have been carried out at least once. For example:

To calculate the sum of:

$1 + \frac{1}{2} + \frac{1}{4} + \frac{1}{8} + \ldots\ldots$

until it differs from 2 by less than 10^{-4}.

Using a WHILE statement:

```
PROGRAM whileexample (output);
CONST epsilon = 1.0e-4;
VAR sum, term : real;
    n           : integer;
BEGIN
sum := 0.0; n := 1;
WHILE abs (2.0 - sum ) >= epsilon DO
   BEGIN
       sum := sum + 1.0 / n;
       n := n + n
   END;
writeln ( sum )
END.
```

Using a REPEAT statement:

```
PROGRAM repeatexample (output);
CONST epsilon = 1.0e-4;
VAR sum, term : real;
    n           : integer;
BEGIN
sum :=0.0 ; n:= 1;
REPEAT
  sum := sum + 1.0/n;
  n := n + n
UNTIL abs (2.0 - sum) < epsilon;
writeln(sum)
END.
```

Exercises

3.1   Write Pascal declarations to set up two integers, hours and minutes. Assuming that values have been given to both variables representing a time in the 24-hour clock, write Pascal statements to convert the time to the 12-hour clock. For example:

if hours is 13
   minutes is 35

change them to give hours is 1
                    minutes is 35

3.2   Modify the preceding question to convert the time to give the simultaneous local time in Singapore (add 7 hours 30 minutes to the time given). Set a `boolean` variable `tomorrow` to `true` if the time in Singapore passes midnight, otherwise `false`.

3.3   Write Pascal declarations and statements to generate successive powers of two (starting at two) until the latest value exceeds 1000.

4

Input and Output

Introduction

Pascal contains statements to enable information to be put into a program and to be transmitted from a program. This chapter is concerned only with the input and output of values expressed as characters. It is possible to transfer values expressed in their internal (binary) form and this is covered later. Although the concepts of input and output are essentially straightforward there are some unfortunate difficulties in Pascal that are concerned with interactive input and output, that is the sort of processing that involves typing data on a keyboard and receiving information on a screen (or printer).

Implementation differences

In standard Pascal (standard Pascal means as defined by Jensen and Wirth) the particular aspects of interactive input and output are not dealt with explicitly (interactive use of computers has grown enormously since the design of Pascal).

One major implementation of Pascal (UCSD) deals with the problems of interactive input and output by redefining the standard statements for performing input and output. This unfortunately makes UCSD a non-standard implementation and raises very serious problems affecting the possible portability of Pascal programs.

Since it is very difficult to discuss standard Pascal and UCSD

Pascal in parallel, this chapter breaks into two parts. Readers using an implementation of Pascal that corresponds to standard Pascal in its input and output should read the parts labelled 'standard', those using UCSD (or similar) should read the parts labelled 'UCSD'. It is possible, though unlikely, that readers may be using an implementation that differs in some respects from both these versions. In that case reading both sections of this chapter and implementation manuals should make the differences clear.

The standard files input and output

Pascal regards all input and output as being from and to 'files'. These may be true files, that is collections of records on disc or tape, or may in fact be streams of characters coming from keyboards or going to printers or screens.

Pascal provides two files automatically; you need not (and must not) declare them yourself.

For input purposes the file input is used. This will refer to either a keyboard or possibly a card-reader or similar device, according to what sort of machine you are using, and in what manner.

For output purposes the file output is used. This will normally refer to a screen but might alternatively be connected to a printer. Other files may be used but must be declared by you.

To use input and output

In standard Pascal you must name the files you intend to use in a program in the program heading. For example:

```
PROGRAM ioexample (input, output, datafile);
```

The files input and output are then accessible to you and have automatically been declared as:

```
VAR input, output : text;
(VAR input, output : interactive;
if using a UCSD system)
```

where text (interactive) is a type automatically declared as:

```
TYPE text = FILE OF char;
(TYPE interactive = FILE OF char;)
```

(Some implementations of Pascal allow input and output to be used without naming them in the program heading, but in such implementations it is usually not an error to do so.)

UCSD does not require the naming of files in the program heading. Doing so, however, is only regarded as an error in early versions.

Reading from standard input

The read statement takes the simplest form:

```
read (v1)
```

where v1 is a variable of type char, integer or real.

1 If the variable is type char:

```
VAR ch : char;
BEGIN
read (ch)
```

this will give to ch the value of the next character on the file input.

2
```
VAR int : integer;
BEGIN
read (int)
```

will skip over spaces and read decimal digits (and an optional + or − sign) to create an integer value. It will stop reading characters after reading the last digit in the sequence.

3
```
VAR r : real;
BEGIN
read (r);
```

will skip leading spaces and read a real value, stopping on the last character that is valid in a real value.

Reading more than one value

A sequence of reads:

```
read (v1); read (v2); read (v3); and so on
```

can be replaced by:

```
read (v1, v2 v3);
```

Dealing with ends of lines (standard Pascal)

Files of type `text` (= `FILE OF char`) are regarded as consisting of lines. The way in which divisions between lines are represented in the file depends upon the implementation in use so Pascal supplies facilities that are independent of such physical divisions.

Ignoring ends of lines (standard Pascal)

If you are not interested in the line structure of the data being read then the continued use of `read` will regard each end-of-line marker as a space and proceed to the next line automatically. If you wish to know when you have reached the end of a line when reading you can use the boolean function `eoln` (end-of-line), which becomes true as soon as the last character on the line (not including the marker) has been read (*not* when the end-of-line marker has been read).

To continue to the next line you can use `read`, which will read the end-of-line marker as a space or `readln`, which skips from the current reading to the beginning of the next line. Both cause `eoln` to be reset to false. `readln` can also be used to skip from the current reading position to the beginning of the next line – thus potentially omitting characters.

The sequence:

```
readln
read (v1);
read (v2);
read (v3);
```

can be replaced by:

```
readln (v1, v2, v3)
```

A convenient schema for processing each character in a line is:

```
VAR ch : char;
BEGIN
    WHILE NOT eoln DO
      BEGIN
          read (ch);
          process (ch)
      END;
    readln
END.
```

Dealing with the end of a file (standard Pascal)

Just as Pascal offers a general technique for dealing with ends of lines it also uses a similar technique for the end of a file. The boolean function eof (end-of-file) becomes true when the last character on the file has been read.

```
PROGRAM countchars (input, output);
(* counts all characters except spaces on input *)
CONST space = ' ';
VAR ch : char;
    count : integer;
BEGIN
    count := 0;
    WHILE NOT eof DO
      BEGIN
         read (ch);
         IF ch <> space
            THEN
               count := count + 1
      END;
    writeln (count) (* see later in chapter *)
END.

PROGRAM linesandchars (input, output);
(* counts characters (not spaces) and lines on
                                      input *)
CONST space = ' ';
VAR count, lines : integer;
    ch : char;
BEGIN
    count := 0;
    lines := 0;
    WHILE NOT eof do
         BEGIN (* through the file *)
            WHILE NOT eoln DO
               BEGIN (* across the line *)
                  read (ch);
                  IF CH <> space
                     THEN
                        count := count + 1
               END; (* eoln *)
            readln; (* skip to next line *)
            lines := lines + 1
         END; (* eof *)
    writeln (lines, count)
END.
```

Reading files other than `input` (standard Pascal)

If you wish to read a file other than standard `input` or in addition to it you must firstly mention its name in the program heading:

```
PROGRAM example (input, output, datafile);
```
(position in list is not important)

Next you must declare it:

```
VAR datafile : text;
```

where `text` is the predefined type `FILE OF char;` In the statements of the program you must use:

```
reset (datafile)
```

before attempting to read the file. This opens the file for reading and positions the reading position at the beginning of the file. Note that `reset (datafile)` can be issued more than once if you wish to read the file more than once in the program. Subsequently, to read from `datafile` it is sufficient to add the name `datafile` as the first parameter of `read` and `readln` and as the (only) parameter of `eoln` and `eof`.

```
PROGRAM list (datafile, output);
(* shows what is in datafile *)
VAR ch : char;
    datafile : text;
BEGIN
    reset (datafile);
    WHILE NOT EOF (datafile) DO
        BEGIN
            WHILE NOT eoln (datafile) DO
                BEGIN
                    read (datafile, ch);
                    write (ch) (* see later *)
                END; (* eoln *)
            writeln; (* see later *)
            readln (datafile)
        END
END.
```

Note that `datafile` is the name of the file so far as the Pascal program is concerned.

Whether `datafile` is the name of the file as far as the operating system is concerned is dependent upon your implementation. To find out how to make the link, if necessary, consult your implementation manual.

To write to standard output (standard Pascal and UCSD)

The write statement in its simplest form is:

```
write (expression)
```

where the expression may be of type:

```
real
integer
char
boolean (not UCSD)
PACKED ARRAY [1..n] OF char (see Chapter 7).
```

A sequence:

```
write (e1); write (e2); write (e3); and so on
```

can be written:

```
write (e1, e2, e3)
```

The number of characters used to express each value e1, e2 and so on is determined by the type of the expression and varies from one implementation to another.

However, it is possible for you to control the minimum number of characters used by supplying an integer expression after the expression to be written. For example:

```
integer: VAR i,k: integer;
```

write (i) writes the value of i using the number of character positions determined by implementation with leading spaces if necessary.

write (i : 4) writes the value of i using four character positions (with leading spaces if necessary).

write (i + 3 : k) writes the value of i + 3 using k character positions.

When working out how many character positions are required, do not forget to include one for the minus sign if the value could be negative.

```
char
```
```
  VAR ch : char;
  write (ch) writes the value of ch using one character position
  write (ch : k + 2) writes the value of ch preceded by
  k + 2 - 1 spaces
```

```
boolean
```
(not UCSD)

```
  VAR truth : boolean;
  write (truth) writes the characters true or false
  write (truth : 7) writes △△△true
  or △△false
  where △ denotes a space
```
```
PACKED ARRAY [1..n] OF char:
```

This type will be covered in depth in Chapter 7. For now you can use it in two ways:

1   Named constants:

```
  CONST name = 'niklaus'
  name is taken to have type:
  PACKED ARRAY [1..7] OF char
```

2   Literal character strings:
    The string 'wirth' is taken to have type:

```
  PACKED ARRAY [1..5] OF char
```

Using these constants in write statements:

```
write (name) will write niklaus using seven character positions
write ('wirth') will write wirth using five character positions
```

```
write ('wirth' : 6)
```
will write △wirth using six character positions where △ denotes a space

```
write (name : 3)
```
will write nik using three character positions

Thus:

```
  write (' ' : 5, name : 3, 'wirth' : 6)
```

will write:

```
nik wirth
```

It is also possible to write variables of type PACKED ARRAY [1..n] OF char (see Chapter 7).

real
> VAR r : real;
> write (r) will write the value of r in decimal floating-point notation using a number of characters determined by the implementation.
> write (r : 15) will write the value of r in decimal floating-point notation using 15 character positions.

When working out how many character positions to allow remember to include:

1 One position for a possible minus sign.
2 Positions for the exponent part.
3 A preceding space (required by language definition).

Although the floating-point notation is useful for scientific work where values may extend over a very great range, a fixed-point notation is more useful in general use. The fixed-point notation is obtained by giving a third expression (integer). For example:

```
r := -27.59427
```
> write (r : 9 : 4) will write the value of r in nine positions in fixed format with four decimal places.
```
- 27.5943 (note rounding)
```

Terminating the line when writing

An end-of-line marker can be placed in the output text by the statement:

```
writeln (write line)
```

The sequence:

```
write (e1); write (e2); write (e3); and so on
writeln
```

can be replaced by:

```
writeln (e1, e2, e3)
```

A writeln with no parameters following another writeln has the effect of placing a blank line in the output text.

A writeln following a write terminates the current line but does not leave a blank line.

Vertical control when writing (standard Pascal and UCSD)

The statement page causes a special character(s) to be sent to the output file or device to cause output to begin on a new page, on a printer or similar effect on a screen. Many implementations (including UCSD) require page (output).

Non-standard vertical control (not UCSD)

Some implementations use a system of vertical control borrowed from FORTRAN. The first character of every output line must be one of four special characters:

- '1' causes current line to appear at the top of the next page (equivalent to page)
- ' ' causes normal vertical spacing to occur
- '0' causes double spacing to occur
- '+' causes over-printing – current line appears on same line as previous one (not normally desirable)

Writing to files other than standard output (standard Pascal)

If you wish to write to a file other than standard output you must first give its name in the program heading:

```
PROGRAM outex (input, output, outfile);
```

then declare it:

```
VAR outfile : text;
```

Before using it, it is necessary to issue:

```
rewrite (outfile)
```

(once only unless you wish to overwrite the file later in the program). This opens the file for writing and sets the mode of access to `write`. To write to the file:

use `write` with a first parameter of `outfile` and `writeln (outfile)` and `page (outfile)`

For example, to copy the file `inp` to the file `out`:

```
PROGRAM copyfile (inp, out, output);
VAR inp, out : text;
    count    : integer;
    ch       : char;
BEGIN
    reset (inp);
    rewrite (out);
    count := 0;
    WHILE NOT eof (inp) DO
      BEGIN
        WHILE NOT eoln (inp) DO
          BEGIN
            read (inp, ch);
            write (out, ch)
          END; (* eoln *)
        writeln (out);
        readln (inp);
        count := count + 1
      END; (* eof *)
    writeln (count :4, ' lines copied');
    writeln ('from file : inp');
    writeln ('to file : out')
END. (* copy file *)
```

Interactive input and output (standard Pascal)

The term *interactive* is used here to indicate a mode of computer processing in which the input to a program is to some extent controlled by its output and the interaction of a user.

A typical situation is that in which a program 'prompts' a user on a screen or printer for input from a keyboard. Pascal in its standard form presents some difficulties regarding the correct synchronisation of input and output.

This is not a fault of the design of Pascal but rather an unfortunate side effect of the generally desirable features of Pascal's input and output.

As you have seen earlier in this chapter, Pascal sets `eoln` to true before reading the end-of-line marker, that is, when it reads the last true character on the line. It also sets `eof` to true before reading the end-of-file marker, that is when it reads the last character of the last line on the file. In order to do this, the Pascal input/output system must in reality be looking at the character one-ahead from the character that you see. It does this by using a 'buffer' or 'window' variable designated filename `^` (or filename @) so the buffer for the file `input` is called `input^` or `input @`.

The statement `reset (filename)` or the implicit `reset (input)` has the effect of loading the first character on the file into the buffer variable. The statement:

    read (ch)

then consists of:

    ch := input^;

which transfers the character currently in the buffer to the variable `ch`, followed by:

    get (input)

which causes the buffer, `input` @, to contain the next character on the file. If the character moved into the buffer by this `get` statement is an end-of-line marker then the character is replaced by a space and `eoln` becomes true.

If the character is an end-of-file character then the buffer is undefined and `eof` becomes true. This system works very well and is the same for all files, not just `input`. It allows the `WHILE NOT eoln DO` and `WHILE NOT eof DO` structures seen in earlier examples.

However, if `input` is connected to a keyboard it becomes tricky since the implicit `reset (input)` occurs before any other statements in the program. `reset` requires a character to be loaded into the buffer but the user will not generally know what to type until he has read the instructions that will be given on `output`.

The situation is further complicated by the fact that many large computer (mainframe) implementations transmit to and from terminals a line at a time.

Thus the implicit `reset` requires the entire first line of input to be loaded into a 'line buffer'. The `read` statements that follow acquire their characters from that line buffer and it will need to be reloaded with the next line when a `readln` is encountered in the program.

Difficulties regarding line buffering can largely be overcome by careful placing of `readln` in your programs. To read pairs of `integer` values, one per line, from standard input and print out their sums:

```
PROGRAM standardinteract (input, output);
VAR val1, val2, sum : integer;
BEGIN
    (* implicit reset (input))
        (and rewrite (output))
        loads first character (or line)*)
    WHILE NOT eof DO
                (* see note in following text *)
        BEGIN
          read (val1, val2);
          sum := val1 + val2;
          writeln (sum : 9 : 4);
          readln (* load next line set eof to
          true if line holds end-of-file marker *)
        END
END. (* standard input *)
```

Note that in the preceding example you need to be able to type an end-of-file marker on your keyboard. This is an implementation-defined character or sequence of characters. Some possibilities are:

```
control c
$eof
++++
$$$
```

You can make the program easier to use by deciding upon your own end-of-file character. Obviously, you must choose a character that could not appear as the first character in a line of normal input. If you wish to regard, say, `'*'` as an end-of-file character you can test for its presence in the buffer for `input` before it is transferred to a variable by a `read` statement. Replace the line:

```
WHILE NOT eof DO
```

by:

```
WHILE input^ <> '*' DO
```

This technique is very useful for making programs portable from one implementation to another. If you wish to allow either the normal (implementation-dependent) end-of-file or your own, write:

```
WHILE NOT eof AND (input^<> '*') DO
```

Possible solutions to the problems caused by implicit `reset (input)`

As you have seen, the implicit `reset (input)` makes it impossible to write out information to guide the user before the system demands some characters to be typed. Solutions to the problem are of two sorts.

Firstly, there are changes to the implementation of input and output (UCSD is so different that it is covered separately):

1   Delay actual loading of the buffer until its value is required or `eof` (or `eoln`) is tested. If you are using such an implementation you need take no further action (called 'lazy' I/O).
2   Supply a compiler directive to require `reset (input)` and `rewrite (output)` to be explicitly stated. Place `reset (input)` after write statements.
3   Fill the buffer automatically with an arbitrary character. The program then discards this character.

Secondly, if none of the first type of solution are available to you, or if you are unable to use them because you require your program to be portable, then you will need to adopt a different approach.

1   Do not use standard `input`. For example:

```
PROGRAM otherinput (myinput, output);
VAR myinput : text;
         ch : char;
BEGIN
     writeln ( ----- );
     writeln ( ----- );
     and so on
     reset (myinput);
     read (myinput, ch); and so on.
```

Arrange for `myinput` to be connected to the keyboard. This is implementation-dependent and is not necessarily possible. You will need to refer to an implementation manual.

2   If none of the preceding methods are available the easiest solution is to instruct all users of your program to type any character(s) and press RETURN (SEND or GO) at the start of your Pascal programs (before seeing anything on `output`). You can then discard these characters. For example:

```
PROGRAM lastditch (input, output);
```

```
BEGIN
    (* implicit reset (input) — user supplies any
        character (as instructed externally) *)
    writeln ( ---- );
    writeln ( ---- );
    writeln ( ---- );
    readln; (* load first real line of data *)
```

Dealing with ends of lines (UCSD Pascal)

Files of type `text` (not from keyboard) are treated precisely as standard Pascal. Interactive devices are treated as type `interactive`. Thus the following automatic declarations can be assumed:

```
TYPE interactive = FILE OF char;
VAR input, keyboard, output : interactive;
```

The difference between types `text` and `interactive` lies in the order of events carried out in performing `read` and `readln` statements and the circumstances that make `eof` and `eoln` true.

The difference between `input` and `keyboard` is that `input` 'echoes' (shows on the screen) what has been typed on the keyboard. Using `keyboard` does not cause echo to appear. 'Files' of type `text` or `interactive` can be thought of as sequences of lines. Lines are terminated by a special 'carriage return' character (called CR in this chapter).

Ignoring ends of lines

If you are not interested in the line structure of the data being read then the continued use of `read` will regard each end-of-line marker as a space and proceed to the next line automatically. If you wish to know when you have reached the end of a line when reading, you can use the boolean function `eoln`, which becomes true *after* the line marker has been read (different from standard). To continue to the next line you can use `read`, which will read the end-of-line marker as a space, or `readln`, which skips from the current reading position to the beginning of the next line. Both cause `eoln` to be reset to false. `readln` can also be used to skip from the current reading position to the beginning of the next line – thus potentially omitting characters.

Dealing with the end of the file (UCSD)

The `boolean` function `eof` (end-of-file) becomes true *after* the special end-of-file marker has been read (different from standard).

```
PROGRAM countchars (input, output); (* UCSD *)
(* counts all characters except spaces on input *)
CONST space = ' ';
VAR ch : char;
    count : integer;
BEGIN
    count := 0;
    read (ch);
    WHILE NOT eof DO
        BEGIN
          IF ch <> space
             THEN
                count := count + 1;
          read (ch)
        END;
    writeln (count)
END.
```

The sequence:

```
read (v1);
read (v2);
read (v3); and so on
readln
```
can be replaced by:

```
readln (v1, v2, v3)
```

A convenient schema for processing each character in a line is:

```
VAR ch : char;
BEGIN
   read (ch);
   WHILE NOT eoln DO
       BEGIN
          process (ch);
          read (ch)
       END;
     readln
END.
```

```
PROGRAM linesandchars (input, output); (* UCSD *)
(* counts characters (not spaces) and lines on
                                      input *)
CONST space = ' ';
VAR count, lines : integer;
    ch : char;
```

```
BEGIN
    count := 0;
    lines := 0;
    read (ch);
    WHILE NOT eof DO
        BEGIN
        WHILE NOT eoln DO
            BEGIN
              IF ch <> space
                THEN
                  count := count + 1;
              read (ch)
            END;
          readln;
          lines := lines + 1;
          read (ch)
        END;
    writeln (lines, count)
END.
```

Conclusion

As you can see, there are potential areas of difficulty here. The only way to cope with these difficulties is to understand why they arise. If the explanation given here does not make everything clear to you, it may help to experiment with some simple interactive programs of your own.

Exercise

4.1 The following program is supposed to be in Pascal. However, it contains syntax errors and semantic errors (errors of logic).

Identify these errors and say which of them you would expect to be detected by the Pascal compiler.

Rewrite the program so that it is correct in syntax and semantics.

```
PROGRAM errors (input, output);
(* finds average of whole numbers *)
(* one per line *)
VAR int total; count;
    real average;
BEGIN
```

```
WHILE NOT eof
      read n;
      total = total + n;
      count = count + 1;
   writeln (' average is', count / total)
END.
```

5

Subranges and Enumeration Types

Ordinal types: a definition

A type is said to be ordinal if it is unstructured (single-valued) and its total number of possible values is finite.

For example, the type `integer` is ordinal since it is always possible to say how many integer values there are in a given range. However, the type `real` is not ordinal since it is always possible to find a real value between any other two reals, however close, and thus the total number of values is infinite. (The type `real` is an approximation to the mathematical type real.)

Subranges

So far you have declared variables in your program to be of four possible types:

```
integer
real
boolean
char
```

However, the values that you may wish to represent in the computer will not always necessarily conform to any of these types.

For example, if you wish to represent the number of minutes past the last hour, you know that this value must lie in the range 0 to 59 inclusive. In most programming languages it is necessary to declare `minutes` to be of type `integer` and it is the programmer's responsibility to avoid absurd values such as −27 and 62. Pascal, however, allows you to declare the type of `minutes` as a subrange (Fig. 5.1).

VAR minutes : 0 ..59;

Fig. 5.1

Now `minutes` can take any integral value in the range 0 to 59 inclusive and any attempt to assign a value outside that range will be indicated as an error either by the compiler, in a case such as:

minutes := 62

or by the runtime diagnostic system:

minutes := expression

In this example, the type of `minutes` is a `subrange` of the type `integer`. `integer` is known as the base type and is deduced from the form of the constants 0 and 59.

Subranges of any ordinal type are permitted. (Note that this excludes subranges of the type `real`.) For example:

VAR numericchars : '0' ..'9' ;

The advantages of subranges are:

1   Runtime diagnostic systems will prevent a value lying outside the subrange being assigned to the variable and will give appropriate messages.
2   The compiler may take advantage of a restricted range by assigning less space for the representation of the value in binary.

It is a good idea always to define variables with the most restrictive possible subrange and thus gain the maximum assistance from the computer in detecting errors.

Enumeration types

If you wish, for example, to represent 'day of the week' as a variable in a program it is normally necessary, in other languages, to declare it to be of type `integer` and then to code the days of the week as numbers, by some arbitrary code. For example:

```
monday = 0 to Sunday = 6
```

It is possible to improve on this by the use of subranges:

```
VAR dayofweek : 0..6;
```

This removes the danger of having a day of week of 7 but does not help with the problem of detecting a weekend:

```
IF (dayofweek = 5) OR (dayofweek = 6)
   THEN
```

Although this is correct it is really not at all obvious that 5 really means Saturday. You could improve upon this by declaring:

```
CONST mon = 0; tues = 1; wed = 2; thurs = 3;
      fri = 4; sat = 5; sun = 6;
```

so then the test becomes:

```
IF (dayofweek = sat) OR (dayofweek = sun)
   THEN
```

This is clearly better but it involves quite a lot of programming effort. This effort can be removed by use of the enumeration type:

```
VAR dayofweek : (mon,tues,wed,thurs,fri,sat,sun);
```

Here, a type is defined by enumerating all its possible values (Fig. 5.2). The values are still coded as integers (in the range 0 to 6) but this fact, which is really of no interest to you, is hidden from you.

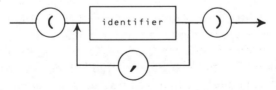

Fig. 5.2

To assign or test values of `dayofweek` you are now only permitted to use the constants in the enumeration list of the definition.

```
IF (dayofweek = sat) OR (dayofweek = sun)
   THEN
```

is now the only correct form:

```
IF (dayofweek = 5) OR (dayweek = 6)
    THEN
```

is syntactically incorrect. Notice that this means it is no longer possible to generate tomorrow's day of the week by adding one to today's day of the week. Instead you must use a special function succ (successor) which gives the next value in an enumeration list. Succ is not defined for the last value in the list.

Pred (predecessor) gives the previous value in the list, (in this case yesterday's day of week) and it is undefined for the first value in the list.

```
VAR yesterday, today, tomorrow:
              (mon,tues,wed,thurs,fri,sat,sun);
```

Given today's value, generate tomorrow's:

```
IF today = sun THEN tomorrow:= mon
               ELSE tomorrow:= succ (today)
```

and to generate yesterday's:

```
IF today = mon THEN yesterday:= sun
               ELSE yesterday:= pred (today)
```

If you ever require to know the underlying integer value given to a variable defined as an enumeration type, this can be obtained by means of the function ord:

```
ord (mon) gives 0
ord (sun) gives 6
```

Note that there is no inverse to ord for use with enumeration types. Enumeration types allow you to declare values without resorting to arbitrary coding as integers. They make programs easier to write and to understand but they are essentially for use *inside* a program and cannot usually be input and output. For example, in colour graphics, a colour might be, defined as:

```
VAR colour : (red,green,blue,white);
```

The TYPE statement

What you have done with subranges and enumeration types is effectively to invent new types. You can give names to these types and then use them just like the standard types. Use the TYPE statement given in Fig. 5.3.

```
TYPE minutetype = 0..59;
     day = (mon,tues,wed,thurs,fri,sat,sun);
VAR minutes : minutetype;
    today,tomorrow: day;
```

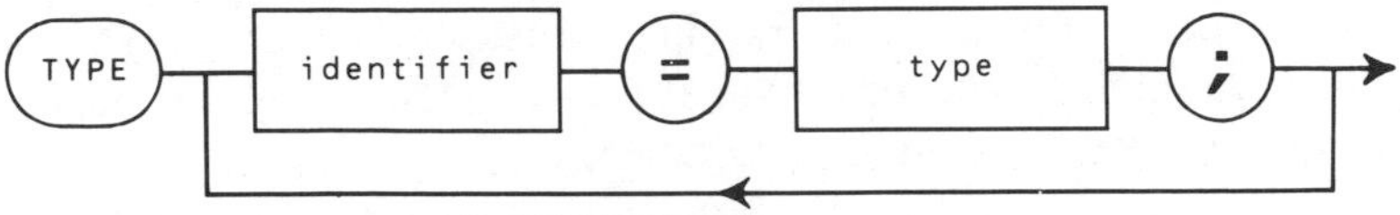

Fig. 5.3

TYPE statements are useful for defining parameters for procedures and functions (see Chapter 9).

The standard constant maxint

There is, for every implementation of Pascal, a standard constant called maxint, which has the value of the largest (positive) value of type integer that can be represented in that implementation.

To discover the value of maxint in your implementation run this program:

```
PROGRAM whatismaxint (output);
BEGIN
  writeln('maxint is',maxint)
END.
```

Maxint is useful in defining types such as:

```
TYPE nonnegative = 0..maxint;
     natural     = 1..maxint;
     toeternity  = 1981..maxint;
```

The type boolean

The standard type boolean is defined as:

```
TYPE boolean = (false,true);
```

thus:

```
ord (false) is 0
ord (true) is 1
```

```
succ (false) is true
pred (true) is false
```

`Boolean` is an enumeration type and is therefore an ordinal type.

Subranges of enumeration types

The declaration of an enumeration type causes the identifiers in the enumeration list to become available as constants. These constants can be used when defining subranges:

```
TYPE day = (mon,tues,wed,thurs,fri,sat,sun);
     workday = mon..fri;
     holiday = sat..sun;
```

To summarise, you can declare subranges of:

```
integer
char
boolean (but it is not useful)
any enumeration type, but not real.
```

Exercises

5.1 Declare a type suitable for representing a year in this century (1900s) as a four-digit `integer`.

5.2 A college has three terms: Michaelmas, Lent and Summer. Declare a type `term` and two variables, `thisterm` and `nextterm`. Write statements to assign a value to `nextterm` given the value of `thisterm`.

6

Further Branching and Looping

Branching – the CASE statement

So far you have used the IF statement for branching. Sometimes you will find that you need to write a series of tests of a variable against various constant values. For example:

```
VAR day : (mon,tues,wed,thurs,fri,sat,sun);
IF day = mon
      THEN write (' monday ')
ELSE IF day = tues
      THEN write (' tuesday ')
ELSE IF day = wed
      THEN write (' wednesday ')
ELSE IF day = thurs
      THEN write (' thursday ')
ELSE IF day = fri
      THEN write (' friday ')
ELSE IF day = sat
      THEN write (' saturday ')
      ELSE write (' sunday ')
```

Pascal provides more convenient syntax for this purpose, in the form of the CASE statement shown in Fig. 6.1. The expression must be of ordinal type. No constant may appear more than once.

The previous example can be rewritten:

```
CASE day OF
  mon:    write (' monday ');
  tues:   write (' tuesday ');
  wed:    write (' wednesday ');
  thurs:  write (' thursday ');
```

```
fri:    write (' friday ');
sat:    write (' saturday ');
sun:    write (' sunday ')
END; (* case *)
```

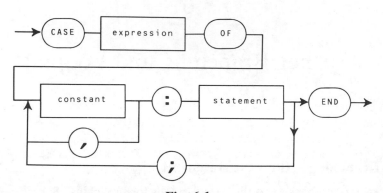

Fig. 6.1

It is a good idea to add the comment (* case *) after END, to remind yourself or another reader of your program, that this END does not have a corresponding BEGIN.

You can use several constants with the same action:

```
CASE day OF
mon, tues, wed,
thurs, fri  : BEGIN
                 dayoff:= false;
                 getuptime := 7
              END;
sat, sun    : BEGIN
                 dayoff:= true;
                 getuptime := 8
              END
END; (* case *)
```

(given suitable declarations for dayoff and getuptime). It is not necessary for the constants to appear in any particular order in the CASE statement.

Failure of expression to match any constant

Frequently, the expression can take more values than you can give matching constants for. This will occur when you use an expression of type char or a large subrange of integer or integer itself. For example:

```
VAR chargecode : char;
    rate        : real;
BEGIN
CASE charcode OF
      'A' : rate := 1.0;
      'B' : rate := 7.5;
      'C' : rate := 15.0;
      'L' : rate := 0.5
END; (* case *)
```

The effect of this CASE statement when charcode has a value other than 'A', 'B', 'C' or 'L' is undefined (Pascal Report).

'Strict' implementations interpret this as meaning that this situation will give rise to a runtime error. This means that you will need to 'protect' the CASE statement with an IF statement:

```
IF (charcode = 'A') OR (charcode = 'B')
   OR (charcode = 'C') OR (charcode = 'D')
   THEN
      CASE charcode OF
```

(and so on)

(or IF charcode IN ['A', 'B', 'C', 'D'] – see Chapter 11).

Other implementations (UCSD in particular) interpret the Pascal Report as meaning that the CASE statement will have no effect in such circumstances. Unfortunately, it then becomes difficult to be certain whether or not the CASE statement has done anything and so further programming, possibly involving IF statements, becomes necessary. Some implementations extend the syntax of Pascal to allow a special section at the end of the list of constants and statements to cover the failure of the expression to match any of the constants. This involves using the reserved word ELSE, or in some cases, OTHERWISE. For example:

```
CASE charcode OF
'A' : --------
'B' : --------
'C' : --------
'L' : --------
OTHERWISE write (' code not recognised ')
END; (* case *)
```

Some extensions require a colon after OTHERWISE. *Note:* use of this option tends to be inefficient in computer terms.

Looping – the FOR statement

Sometimes it is necessary to write a loop that is repeated a fixed number of times. For example, to find the sum of the squares of the first 50 whole numbers:

```
VAR sum,n : integer;
BEGIN
SUM := 0;
n := 1;
WHILE n <= 50 DO
   BEGIN
     sum := sum + sqr(n);
     n := n + 1
   END; (* while *)
writeln (sum)
```

The FOR statement makes this sort of loop simpler to write as is shown in Fig. 6.2. The previous example could be rewritten:

```
sum := 0;
FOR n := 1 TO 50 DO
    sum := sum + sqr(n);
writeln (sum)
```

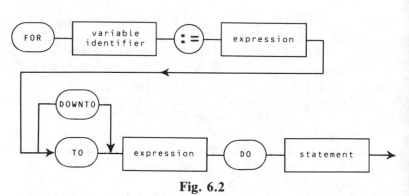

Fig. 6.2

The variable must be of ordinal type, the expressions must be of the same type as the variable and the statement can be a compound statement.

The FOR loop can be used effectively with enumeration types. If TO is used then the succ function is applied to the variable to generate the next value, if DOWNTO then the pred function is applied.

It is not possible to cause the loop to step up (or down) by amounts other than 1 (or −1).

Additionally, it is not possible to use a FOR loop on real variables. This would be inadvisable in any case for reasons of accuracy. To take two examples:

1   To print values of sqrt (x) for values of x from 0.0 to 1.0 in steps of 0.1:

```
VAR i : integer;
    x : real;
BEGIN
FOR i := 0 TO 10 DO
   BEGIN
      x := i/10.0;
      write (x : 4 : 1, sqrt (x) : 8 : 6)
   END
```

2   To print a truth table for the boolean expression a OR (b AND c):

```
PROGRAM truthtable (output);
VAR a, b, c : boolean;
BEGIN
   writeln('a':6, 'b':6, 'c':6, 'a OR (b and c)')
   FOR a := false TO true DO
   FOR b := false TO true DO
   FOR c := false TO true DO
      writeln (a:6, b:6, c:6, a OR (b AND c):6)
END.
```

Note that in UCSD Pascal you will need to replace each part of the writeln (boolean value) by:

```
IF boolean  value
THEN write ('true':6)
ELSE write ('false':6);
```

Unstructured transfer of control – the GOTO statement

The branching and looping statements of Pascal have largely rendered the GOTO statement (as used in FORTRAN, BASIC, COBOL and other languages) unnecessary. However, there are some rare situations in which it is necessary to use it. It has the form as shown in Fig. 6.3. A label should appear at the beginning of a line.

It is necessary to declare all labels used in a program. This precedes the declaration of constants as in Fig. 6.4. For example:

```
PROGRAM usesGOTO (input, output);
LABEL 99;
CONST pi = 3.14159;
...
BEGIN
...
IF eof THEN GOTO 99; (* unexpected end of file *)
...
99:
END.
```

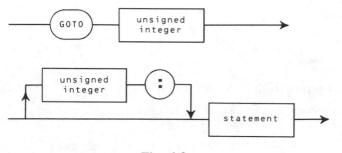

Fig. 6.3

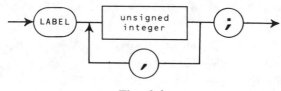

Fig. 6.4

In UCSD Pascal it is necessary to give a compiler directive before attempting to use labels or GOTO statements. This is to discourage indiscriminate use of GOTOs.

When to use GOTO statements

It is rarely necessary to use GOTO statements in Pascal programs. Excessive use of them frequently indicates that the branching and looping statements of Pascal are not being used to full advantage. The best rule to follow is to use GOTO statements only to deal with

unusual situations that break the normal control structure of a
program, for example, discovering an unexpected end-of-file.

Exercises

Note that GOTO statements are *never* needed in solutions to the
exercises in this book.

6.1 Write a Pascal program to print the values 10, 9, 8, 7, 6, 5, 4, 3,
2, 1, in that order, one to a line. Use a FOR loop.

6.2 Write a Pascal program to evaluate:

$$y = 261.378 \text{ times } \sqrt{1 + x^2}$$

for values of x:

1.00, 1.01, 1.02, ... 3.00

printing out pairs (x, y) one per line.

6.3 The Pascal program that follows reads sets of three co-
efficients:

a, b, c of quadratic equations:

$$y = ax^2 + bx + c$$

and states the sort of roots that each equation has. (Roots are
values of x for which $y = 0$.)

If a is zero and b is zero then there is no solution, but if b is
not zero then there is one root.

If a is not zero then the sort of root is determined from the
'discriminant':

If the discriminant is positive then the roots are real.
If the discriminant is zero then the roots are coincident.
If the discriminant is negative then the roots are complex.

Unfortunately, the person who wrote this program was not
properly familiar with the sequence control constructs of
Pascal and the program looks more like FORTRAN.

Rewrite the program making good use of the appropriate
constructs of Pascal. There is no need to use GOTOs or LABELs.

```
PROGRAM messyquad (input, output);
(* sort of roots equation ax2 + bx + c has *)
```

```
LABEL 1,2, 3, 4, 5, 6;
CONST eps = 1.0e-10;
(* tolerance - absolute values smaller*)
(* than this are treated as zero *)
VAR    a,b,c, discr : real;
       count : integer;
BEGIN
       count := 0;
   1:  IF eof THEN GOTO 6;
       readln (a,b,c);
       write (a,b,c);
       count:=count + 1;
       IF abs(a)<eps THEN GOTO 2;
       discr := sqr(b) - 4.0*a*c;
       IF discr > eps THEN GOTO 4;
       IF discr < -eps THEN GOTO 5;
       writeln (' coincident roots ');
       GOTO 1;
   2:  IF abs(b)<eps THEN GOTO 3;
       writeln ('single root ');
       GOTO 1;
   5:  writeln(' complex roots ');
       GOTO 1;
   3:  writeln (' no solution ');
       GOTO 1;
   4:  writeln(' real roots ');
       GOTO 1;
   6:  writeln (' no. of records processed = ', count)
END. (* messyquad *)
```

6.4   Write a Pascal program to assign the correct number of days in
      the month to a variable, given a month. Use the declarations
      as below:

```
VAR leap : boolean;
    daysinmonth : 1..31;
    month : (jan, feb, mar, apr, may, jun,
             jul, aug, sep, oct, nov, dec);
```

Use a CASE statement. Assume that leap is true if the year is
a leap year.

7

A Structured Type – the ARRAY

The concept of an array

So far, the only types of data used have been scalars; that is, single values. Frequently, however, it is necessary to represent a series of values of the same type. For example, it may be necessary to represent rainfall figures for each month of a year. This could be done by declaring:

```
VAR      janrf, febrf, marrf,
         aprrf, mayrf, junrf,
         julrf, augrf, seprf,
         octrf, novrf, decrf : real;
```

However, most processing using these values will be rather tedious and it will, for example, be very difficult to write a program to give the total rainfall for the year up until a given month.

An alternative is to use an array. This is a series of values of the same type referred to by a single name (Fig. 7.1). The required

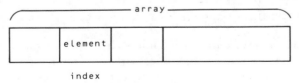

Fig. 7.1

element of an array is selected by means of a value called an index (or subscript) of ordinal type, which follows the array name in square brackets (Fig. 7.2). For example:

```
TYPE monthype = ( jan, feb, mar, apr,
                  may, jun, jul, aug,
                  sep, oct, nov, dec );
VAR  rainfall : ARRAY [ monthype ] OF real;
     thismonth,
     finalmonth : monthype;
     total : real;
BEGIN
     finalmonth := aug; (*for example*)
     total := 0.0;
     FOR thismonth := jan TO finalmonth DO
         total := total + rainfall [ thismonth ];
END.
```

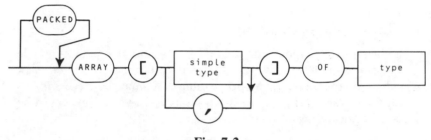

Fig. 7.2

The index type of an array may be;

subrange of integer

```
char
boolean
```
enumeration type

For reasons of size:

```
ARRAY [integer] OF ...
```

is not allowed since this would imply an array for which any integer can be a valid index. Since there are very many possible integer values the resulting array would be very large. The *element* type of an array may be any type, including an array type. (Many implementations forbid:

```
ARRAY [index] OF FILE OF ...
```

which would imply an array of files.)

Two-dimensional arrays (ARRAYS of ARRAYS)

In mathematics a very useful construction is the matrix. This is a two-dimensional array of real values. This can be declared in Pascal as:

```
CONST rows = 5; columns = 3;
TYPE matrix5by3 =
        ARRAY [1..rows] OF
        ARRAY [1..columns] OF real;
VAR i, j : integer;
       a : matrix5by3;
```

Elements of the matrix can be referenced by:

```
a [i] [j]
```

If i and j are declared as:

```
i : 1..rows;
j : 1..columns;
```

there is no danger of either index ever being out of range.

The syntax of multi-dimensional arrays is rather tedious so it can be replaced by an abbreviated form. For example:

```
ARRAY [1..rows] OF ARRAY [1..columns] OF real
```

can be written:

```
ARRAY [1..rows,1..columns] OF real
```

and the referencing of a as:

```
a[i,j]
```

Examples of array declarations and references

```
TYPE posint = 0..maxint;
     betweenwars = 1919..1938;
VAR  unemployed : array [betweenwars] OF posint;
     year       : betweenwars;
     posvar     : posint;
     intvar     : integer;
```

To refer to unemployed:

```
unemployed[year]
```

It is permissible to refer to unemployed using posvar as an index:

```
unemployed[posvar]
```

but this will need a runtime check to ensure that the value of posvar lies in the range 1919 <=posvar <=1938. Similar considerations apply to the use of:

```
unemployed[intvar]
```

No such checks are needed if year is used.

Further examples include declarations

```
TYPE quarter = (first, second, third, fourth);
     figures = ARRAY [quarter] OF integer;
     period  =1976..1980;
VAR  profits, losses, turnover : figures;
     fiveyearprofits : ARRAY [period] OF figures;
     current : quarter;
```

References:

profits for second quarter:

```
profits [second]
```

turnover for third quarter:

```
turnover [third]
```

losses for current quarter:

```
losses [current]
```

profits for first quarter of 1977

```
fiveyearprofits [1977] [first]
```

or:

```
fiveyearprofits [1977,first]
```

Declarations:

```
TYPE vote = (nay,aye);
     tally = 0..maxint;
VAR results : ARRAY [vote] OF tally;
```

References:

```
IF results [nay] > results [aye]
   THEN
    write ('the nays have it')
   ELSE
    IF results [aye] > results [nay]
       THEN
         write ('the ayes have it')
```

```
        ELSE
          write ('draw!')
```

Compatibility of arrays

Arrays of the same type may be assigned to each other. To be of the same type arrays must have the same index type (if subranges they must be identical) and the same element type. Only arrays of identical type PACKED ARRAY [1..n] OF char may be compared with each other.

PACKED ARRAYS

The reserved word PACKED can be put in front of the word ARRAY in any array declaration to indicate to the compiler the programmer's preference that the array should be organised to take up as little space as possible in the computer's store.

This may well incur a cost in terms of reduced speed of access to the array. Precisely what is done by the compiler is determined by the implementation and depends upon the design of the computer. In some implementations PACKED is ignored altogether.

```
VAR apacked : PACKED ARRAY [1..4] OF real;
    aunpacked : ARRAY [1..4] OF real;
```

apacked cannot be assigned to aunpacked or vice versa. However:

```
aunpacked [3] := apacked [3]
```

is permissible.

To make assignments easier there are two special procedures, pack and unpack.

```
pack ( (*from*) a,
       (*starting at*) i, (*in a*)
       (*into*) b )
unpack ( (*from,*) b,
         (*into*) a,
         (*starting at*) i (*in a*) )
```

where a is an unpacked array and b is a packed array of suitable index range and element type. *Note:* many implementations, including UCSD, omit pack and unpack.

Strings of characters (standard Pascal)

In standard Pascal strings of characters are regarded as being of type:

```
PACKED ARRAY [1..n] OF char;
```

where n is an integer constant and is the number of characters in the string. Thus 'PASCAL' is of type:

```
PACKED ARRAY [1..6] OF char;
```

The write statement can write such character strings (see Chapter 4) and they can be assigned to each other following the same rules for arrays in general:

```
VAR name : PACKED ARRAY [1..10] OF char;
name := 'pascal    ';
```

In addition, strings of equal length can be compared using the six relational operators. For example:

```
IF name = 'pascal    '
    THEN
IF name < 'pascal    '
    THEN
```

The comparison takes place using the numeric code values of the characters and works character-by-character from left to right. (Be careful when using implementations that use character codes that are not continuous ranges, such as EBCDIC.)

Strings in UCSD Pascal (and some other implementations)

As you have seen, standard Pascal allows strings only in a rather restrictive form. UCSD Pascal provides an extra standard type string. Variables can be declared as:

```
VAR name : string;
```

This allows a variable-length string of characters of up to 80 characters.

If you wish to have a maximum length of more or less than this, you can declare:

```
string [n]
```

where n is a constant not greater than 255. For example:

```
VAR carreg : string [7];
    printline : string [132];
```

Variables of type string can be assigned the value of any shorter or equal string. For example:

```
carreg := 'abc123x'
```

or

```
carreg := 'aa1'
```

Strings of different lengths can be compared. For example:

'cab' is 'less than' 'cable'.

Note that:

'cab' is not equal to 'cab '.

Strings can be indexed to give a character. The index must not exceed the current length of the string. For example:

```
VAR name : string;
    ch   : char;
name := 'kenneth';
ch := name [6];
```
gives the value 't' to ch

String handling functions and procedures in UCSD Pascal

UCSD Pascal provides several useful functions and procedures for manipulating variables of type string. The most useful of these are as follows:

1   length (string)

which gives the current (integer) length of a string given in brackets. For example:

```
VAR name : string [20];
    l    : integer;
    name := 'edsger';
    l := length (name);
```

gives l the value 6.

```
l := length ('');
```

gives l the value 0.

2 `concat (string, string, ..string)`

Joins together (concatenates) any number of strings to produce a single string. For example:

```
VAR a, d, p, z : string;
a := 'algorithms';
d := 'data structures';
p := 'programs';
z := concat ( a, '+', d, '=', p );
```

gives z the value:

```
algorithms+data structures=programs.
```

3 `pos (substring, string)`
gives the position value of the first occurrence of a substring within a string. For example:

```
VAR l : integer;
    authors : string;
authors := 'jensen and wirth';
l := pos ('and', authors);
```

gives l the value 8.

```
l := pos ('und', authors);
```

gives l the value 0 to indicate that the substring `'und'` could not be found in the string `authors`.

4 `copy (string, start position, length)`
gives a substring from the string given its starting position and length. For example:

```
VAR authors, designer : string;
authors := 'jensen and wirth';
designer := copy (authors, 12, 5);
```

gives `designer` the value `'wirth'`.

5 `insert (string, (*into*), string, (*at*) position)`
inserts a string within another at a given position.

```
VAR names : string;
names := 'jensen wirth';
insert ('and ', names, 8);
```

gives `names` the value:

```
'jensen and wirth'.
```

6 delete ((*from*) string, position, length)
   removes length characters from the string starting at position.
   For example:

```
VAR names : string;
names := 'jensen and wirth';
delete (names, 7, 10);
```

gives names the value:

```
'jensen'.
```

For further details refer to a UCSD Pascal reference manual.

Exercises

7.1 Write a complete Pascal program to read any number of real
     values from a file (one per line), to calculate their mean
     average and to write out all those that were above average.
     Ignore any values after the first 100.

7.2 Declare a type 'matrix' with three rows and five columns of
     real elements.
     Declare three matrices a, b and c and, assuming that values
     have been assigned to a and b, write statements to generate
     values for c such that each element of c is the sum of the
     corresponding elements of a and b.

7.3 Use the array declared as:

```
VAR pass : ARRAY [boolean] OF integer;
```

to count the number of exam marks that constitute passes and
those that are fails. The marks are of type integer, one to a
line and the passmark is 40.

7.4 Write a Pascal program to count separately the occurrences of
     the letters 'a' to 'z' in a file of characters. Ignore end-of-line
     markers and characters that are not letters. Print out the
     frequency of each letter. Assume that the letters 'a' to 'z'
     form a continuous range.

8

A Structured Type – the RECORD

The concept of a RECORD

The RECORD structure in Pascal is another structured type. It differs from the ARRAY in that its components may be of different types (Fig. 8.1).

Note: it is usually an error to put a semi-colon before the END in a RECORD declaration.

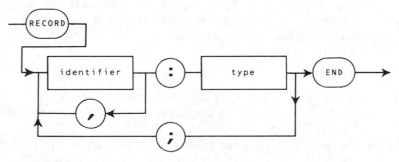

Fig. 8.1

An everyday example of the use of a RECORD structure is the date. This could be expressed in Pascal as:

```
VAR date : RECORD
           day : 1..31;
           month : 1..12;
           year : 1900..1999 (* no semi-colon *)
           END; (* date *)
```

Thus it is possible to regard the date as a single entity.

In order to select a component from a RECORD structure the syntax shown in Fig. 8.2 is used. For example:

```
date.day := 15;
date.month := 2;
date.year := 1981;
```

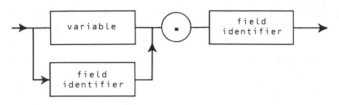

Fig. 8.2.

Since a RECORD structure constitutes a new type it can be used in a position where a type appears – so:

```
TYPE datetype = RECORD
                day : 1..31;
                month : 1..12;
                year : 1900..1999
               END; (* datetype *)
```

Furthermore, you can use RECORD structures as components of other RECORD structures, either explicitly or by using a named type, as in this example:

```
VAR friend : RECORD
             name : PACKED ARRAY [1..10] OF char;
             birthday : datetype
             END;
friend.name := 'CHRIS      ';
friend.birthday.day := 6;
```

RECORD structures can be used as the element types of ARRAYS, as in:

```
ARRAY [1..4] OF date;
ARRAY [1..4] OF RECORD
                codeno : integer;
                currentlevel : real
                END;
```

and ARRAYS can be used as components of RECORDS.

```
RECORD
    name : PACKED ARRAY [1..10] OF char;
    codenumber : PACKED ARRAY [1..6] OF char
END;
```

The WITH statement

As you can see, the names of components of RECORD structures within RECORD structures become rather complicated and tedious. To overcome this, Pascal offers the WITH statement (Fig. 8.3). This effectively qualifies the name, where appropriate, so that you can replace the code of the previous example by:

```
WITH friend DO
  BEGIN
      name := 'CHRIS      ';
    birthday.day := 6;
    birthday.month := 12;
  END; (* with friend *)
```

or better still:

```
WITH friend DO
  BEGIN
      name := 'CHRIS      ';
      WITH birthday DO
        BEGIN
          day := 6;
          month := 12;
          ...
        END; (* with birthday *)
  END; (* with friend *)
```

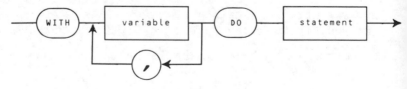

Fig. 8.3

If you find yourself writing something of the form:

```
WITH friend DO
  WITH birthday DO
```

then note that this can be replaced by:

```
WITH friend, birthday DO
```

Note also that this is different from:

```
WITH friend.birthday DO
```

which would qualify all references to variables with:

```
friend.birthday
```

which would not be suitable for name, which would then be regarded as being unqualified.

Further examples of RECORD structures

```
TYPE complex = RECORD
                 re, im, : real
               END; (* complex *)
     cartesian = RECORD
                 x, y : real
               END; (* cartesian *)
     polar = RECORD
                 radius, angle : real
               END; (* polar *)
```

PACKED records

The prefix PACKED can be applied to a RECORD structure as it is to an ARRAY. It does not affect the meaning of the RECORD structure, only the way it is laid out in the store in the machine.

The compiler will usually try to fit a PACKED RECORD structure into less space in the computer's store, possibly incurring an additional penalty in terms of the time taken to reference the RECORD's components.

A useful construction using RECORDS

To simulate variable-length strings (these are already available in UCSD Pascal):

```
CONST maxlen = 10; (* for example *)
      space  = ' ';
```

```
TYPE   variable = RECORD
                      currl : 0..maxlen;
                      value : PACKED ARRAY
                                  [1..maxlen] OF char
                  END; (* variable *)
VAR vstring : variable;
    i : 1..maxlen;
```

To read a 'variable' string (at the end of a line):

```
WITH vstring DO
  BEGIN currl:= 0;
    FOR i := 1 TO maxlen DO
      IF eoln
          THEN
             value [i] := space
          ELSE
             BEGIN
                currl := i;
                read (value [i])
             END
  END; (* with *)
  readln
```

To write a 'variable' string:

```
WITH vstring DO
        write (value : currl)
```

RECORDS with variants

So far all the RECORDs you have seen have had a fixed structure. It is, however, possible to allow alternative structures (variants) within records (Fig. 8.4).

Variants are used when a single, fixed structure may not be appropriate. For example, to record details of a journey (across the channel) that can be made either by air, hovercraft or boat, certain information such as duration, departure time and arrival time may be invariant. Other information may depend upon the mode of travel. This can be represented as follows:

```
TYPE time = RECORD
                hours : 0..23;
                minutes : 0..59
                END; (* time *)
     duration = 0..24; (* hours *)
     airportcode = (BRV, CDG, ORY, AMS, RTM, BHX,
                LGW, LHR, LTN, )*et cetera*));
```

```
         airlinecode = (BA, (* et cetera *) ;
         port = (Dover, Folkestone, Ramsgate, Ostend,
                 Calais, Zeebrugge);
VAR travel : RECORD
             (* invariant part *)
             journeytime : duration;
             starttime,
             endtime : time;
             (* variant part *)
             CASE mode : (air, hovercraft, boat) OF
             air : (depairport,
                 arrairport : airportcode;
                 airline : airlinecode );
             hovercraft,
             boat : ( depport,
                   arrport : port )
             END; (* travel *)
```

Note that the variant part must come after the fixed (invariant) part. (Variants may themselves contain variant parts that must also obey the above rule.)

The variant part must be introduced by use of the CASE statement in which a tag-field, in this case mode, is declared. In this example, mode is given an enumeration type but it can be of any ordinal type.

Field list

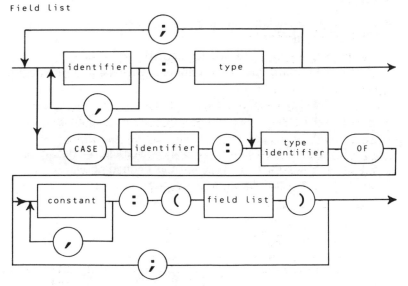

Fig. 8.4

The value of this tag-field determines which variant is currently applicable.

To avoid ambiguity one variant may not have any components that have the same name as components of other variants.

Variants without tag-fields

The normal method of using variant records involves the use of a tag-field that immediately precedes the variant part and explicitly dictates, by its value, which variant is applicable for a given record.

In certain circumstances, it may not be possible to include a tag-field and the appropriate variant may have to be deduced from the nature of the contents of the variant part. In such circumstances the tag-variable may be omitted (though its type is still declared). It is the programmer's responsibility to avoid the confusion that can easily arise in such a situation.

It is inadvisable to take advantage of this possibility of omission until you are a very experienced Pascal programmer.

Exercises

8.1 Write type declarations to set up new types to the following requirements.

(*a*) A subscript in the range 1 to 10.

(*b*) A month name as an enumeration type (abbreviated if you like).

(*c*) A day (expressed as a number).

(*d*) A date, using day and month as above and an integer for year.

(*e*) A person, consisting of name (10 characters), date of birth and date of death (use date as defined above).

Declare a variable of type person and write assignment statements to give the following values to it:

name:　　　　　Pascal
date of birth:　　19th June 1623
date of death: 19th August 1662

8.2 It is required to represent information about students on courses on a file. There will be two variants of the record type distinguished by a tag-field s t a f f (true or false). Assuming the following declarations:

```
TYPE code = PACKED ARRAY [1..5] OF char;
     line = PACKED ARRAY [1..25] OF char;
```

write a Pascal declaration to set up the record description as follows:

field-name	description
name	line
jobtitle	line
staff	true or false
dept	code ⎫
location	code ⎬ staff only
charge-code	code ⎭
manager	line ⎫ not staff
company name	line ⎭
address	three lines

9

Functions and Procedures

Standard functions

You have already met the standard functions provided in Pascal (sin, sqrt and so on). Clearly these functions do a great deal of work but this is hidden from you.

These functions allow you to concentrate on the process that you are trying to program without worrying about the details of, for example, finding a square-root.

Secondly, the use of a function saves duplication of programming if the same process is required several times in a program.

Writing your own functions

Pascal provides a minimum of standard functions but allows you to declare new functions of your own and then use them in exactly the same way as you use standard functions (Fig. 9.1). Function (and procedure) declarations appear after any VAR declarations and before the first BEGIN of their surrounding program (or function or procedure). For example, you might find it useful in a particular program to have a function to obtain the cube of a given real value.

```
FUNCTION cube (x : real) : real;
(* returns x cubed *)
BEGIN
   cube := x * x * x
END; (* cube *)
```

This function is called cube. It needs one parameter of type real,

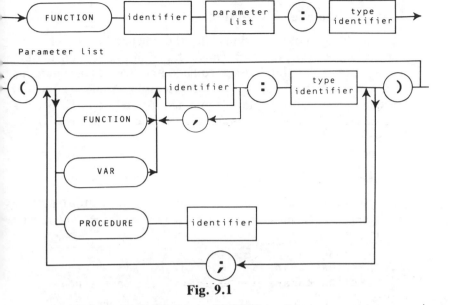

Parameter list

Fig. 9.1

(see later for notes on UCSD and BSI Pascal)

identified within the function by the name x. It returns a value of
type real given by the assignment to cube.

Examples of using the function cube

```
x := cube (6.7)
y := cube (x)
z := cube (y + 2.5) * 7.2
z := cube (cube (x))

PROGRAM testcube (output);
VAR i : integer;
    r : real;
FUNCTION cube (x : real) : real;
BEGIN (* cube *)
    cube := x * x * x
END; (* cube *)
BEGIN (* testcube *)
    FOR i:=1 TO 10 DO
            BEGIN
            r := i/10.0;
            writeln (r:4:1, cube (r) : 9:3)
            END (* for *)
END. (* testcube *)
```

The structure of a function

The declaration of a function (after the function heading) has the same format as a program. Thus a function can contain LABEL, CONST, TYPE, VAR (and FUNCTION and PROCEDURE) declarations. Such declarations are only 'in scope' (accessible) while the function is being executed or while a 'contained' procedure or function is being executed. Their values are not preserved from one call of the function to the next.

The return type of a function may be a scalar type, that is:

integer, real, char, boolean, enumeration type,

or a subrange of any of these. It can also be a pointer type (see Chapter 13). It must be given as a type identifier *not* a type definition:

```
TYPE nonneg = 0..maxint;
FUNCTION noparams : nonneg; is valid
FUNCTION noparams : 0..maxint; is not valid
```

The parameters of a function may be of any type. The type must be given by a type identifier:

```
FUNCTION oneparam (i : nonneg ) : boolean;
```

is valid.

```
FUNCTION oneparam (i : 0..maxint) : boolean;
```

is not valid.

Exercises on functions

9.1   Write a boolean function called alphabetic which accepts a PACKED ARRAY of 10 characters as a parameter and returns true if every character is either 'A'–'Z' or a space and otherwise returns false.

9.2   Write a function called areaofcircle which accepts the radius of a circle as its parameter and returns the area of the circle.

area = πr^2

where π is 3.1415926536 (approximately), r is radius.

Procedures

Procedures are the same as functions in all respects except that:

1 A procedure does not return a value through its name.
2 A procedure heading begins with the word PROCEDURE in place of FUNCTION (Fig. 9.2).

Fig. 9.2

As you have seen, a function can (and must) return one value that is of limited type. Sometimes you will not want to return any value, or you may wish to return more than one, or return a value of a structured type.

Examples of procedures with no parameters

```
PROCEDURE newpage;
CONST heading = 'pascal programming';
      centred = 40;
BEGIN
      page (output);
      writeln (heading : centred)
END; (* newpage *)
```

To use newpage:

```
IF linecount > pagedepth
   THEN
     BEGIN
         newpage;
         linecount := 1
     END;
```

Procedures with parameters

Alternatively, the procedure can receive a parameter value:

```
PROCEDURE newpage (pageno : integer);
CONST heading = 'pascal program';
      centred = 40;
      right   = 'page';
```

```
BEGIN
    page (output);
    writeln(heading : centred, 'page' : right,
                                    pageno : 4)
END; (* newpage *)
```

To use:

```
VAR pnumber, linecount : integer;
    pnumber := 1;
    newpage (pnumber);
    IF linecount > pagedepth
    THEN BEGIN
        pnumber := pnumber + 1;
        newpage (pnumber);
        linecount := 1
        END;
```

Passing values back through parameters

So far all the parameters used in examples of functions and procedures have been 'value' parameters. This means that when a parameter has been stated in a function heading or procedure heading, a value of the given type is required when the function or procedure is used; this means that constants or expressions can be given as parameters when using functions or procedures. In effect, the parameter identifier holds a copy of the supplied parameter value. This method is good for passing parameter values into functions or procedures, but it does not allow the value of a parameter to be changed.

To make this possible the parameter identifier in the function or procedure heading must be preceded by the reserved word VAR. This makes the parameter a variable (or reference) parameter. Now the procedure requires the name of a variable (or element of array or component of record) to be supplied.

The procedure then has a reference to that variable and can work on it directly, changing its value if desired. Thus constants or expressions must not be supplied as actual parameters to match variable parameters.

The use of VAR parameters with functions is permissible but not recommended. For example:

```
PROCEDURE incr (VAR i : integer);
```

```
BEGIN
    i := i + 1
END; (* incr *)
```

To use:

```
incr (count)
incr (total [errors])
```

but not:

```
incr (2)
```

Note: it is *not* permissible to pass elements of PACKED arrays or components of PACKED records as parameters that are declared with VAR. This simplifies the implementation of the mechanism for passing parameters.

A secondary use of VAR parameters

As you have seen, declaring a parameter without using the word VAR results in a copy of the supplied parameter being made.

Sometimes the parameter is of a structured type and occupies a large amount of computer store (for example, an array or record structure).

For this reason it may be more efficient in terms of computer space and time to avoid making a copy (even if the structure is not to be changed). This can be done by declaring the parameter with VAR:

```
PROCEDURE example (VAR unchanged : hugestructure);
```

Files as parameters

If an object of type FILE OF (text means FILE OF char) is to be passed as a parameter it must always be a VAR parameter. (Omission of VAR, if permitted, would imply that a copy of the file must be passed.) For example:

```
PROGRAM usesfiles (datain, dataout);
VAR datain, dataout : text;

PROCEDURE open (VAR inp, out : text);
```

```
BEGIN
  reset (inp);
  rewrite (out)
END; (* open *)

BEGIN (* main program *)
  open (datain, dataout);
```

Exercise on procedures

9.3 Write a procedure a r e a a n d c i r c that accepts the radius of a
     circle as its first parameter and returns the circle's area and
     circumference in its second and third parameters.

> Circumference $= 2\pi r$
> where r is the radius

Using declared objects not passed as parameters

The scope rules of Pascal make it possible for procedures and
functions to have access to objects declared in the surrounding
program (or procedure or function) unless there is another object
with the same name declared locally.

Note: in UCSD a GOTO statement cannot go to a label that is not
declared within the same function or procedure. This means you
cannot jump out of a function or procedure. The EXIT statement is
provided for this purpose. It is *never* permissible to jump into a
procedure or function.

The scope of functions and procedures

A function or procedure can call another function or procedure
declared at the same level so long as the declaration of the called
function or procedure precedes that of the calling function or
procedure.

```
PROGRAM MAIN;

PROCEDURE x;
BEGIN
    (* x cannot call y *)
END; (* x *)

PROCEDURE y;
```

```
BEGIN
     x (* y can call x *)
END; (* y *)
```

This point is discussed later in this chapter.

In general, it is very useful to be able to make reference to the constants, types and variables from the surrounding body. However, it is generally not advisable to change the value of variables that are not locally declared.

Although this is permissible, it has the disadvantage that the function or procedure may have unforeseen 'side-effects' as demonstrated (in an exaggerated manner) in the following example:

```
PROGRAM bizarre (output);
VAR x, y, a: real;
FUNCTION horrid (x : real) : real;
BEGIN
     horrid := sqr (x);
     a := a + 1.0 (* side effect *)
END; (* horrid *)
BEGIN (* bizarre *)
     x := 1.0;
     a := 5.0;
     y := horrid (x) + a;
     writeln (y);              (* writes 7 *)
     x := 1.0;
     a := 5.0;
     y := a + horrid (x);
     writeln (y)              (* writes 6 *)
END. (* bizarre *)
```

Since Pascal compilers normally cause expressions to be evaluated left to right (after precedence rules have been taken into account) the writeln statements will usually cause the values indicated to be written.

Deciding whether to use parameters or to take advantage of scope

This problem will be illustrated by the following example. In most programs it is necessary to give initial values to variables and perform other initialisation work. This can conveniently be done in a procedure. It is for you to choose which of the following approaches is preferable in particular circumstances.

```
PROGRAM usescope;
VAR a, b, c : integer;
    start : boolean;
PROCEDURE initialise;
    BEGIN
       a := 0;
       b := 0;
       c := 0;
       start := true
    END; (* initialise *)
BEGIN (* use scope *)
   initialise;
   (* et cetera *)
END. (* usescope *)
```

This is quick to write but has the disadvantage that you cannot be sure what initialisation is performed by initialise without looking up the procedure body.

```
PROGRAM withparams;
VAR a,b,c :integer;
    start : boolean;
PROCEDURE initialise (VAR x,y,z : integer;
                      VAR b : boolean);
BEGIN (* initialise *)
   x := 0;
   y := 0;
   z := 0;
   b := true
END; (* initialise *)
BEGIN (* withparams *)
   initialise (a,b,c, start);
   (* et cetera *)
END. (* with params *)
```

This second approach may seem tedious, but it has the advantage, particularly in a large program, of making it clear to the reader which variables are being initialised and is thus likely to lead to more correct programming.

Recursion

Recursion is a programming technique that depends upon the ability of a procedure or function to call itself. This is not (normally) available in languages such as BASIC, FORTRAN or COBOL. It is particularly valuable when used in conjunction with *dynamic* data structures (see Chapter 13).

An example of recursion – the factorial function

The classical example of a recursive definition is that of the mathematical concept of a factorial. This is defined for the natural numbers (positive integers) such that factorial of *n* is *n* multiplied by all its predecessors. For example:

Factorial 5 (written 5!) is 5×4×3×2×1 (120)
Factorial 6 (6!) is 6×5×4×3×2×1 (720)

Note that 6! = 6 × 5!

It is a general property of factorials that:

$n! = n \times (n - 1)!$
(1! is defined to be 1)

Thus the factorial property can be defined in terms of itself. It is said to be 'recursively' defined.

It is possible to take advantage of this to write a function in Pascal:

```
TYPE natural = 1..maxint;
FUNCTION factorial (n : natural):natural;
BEGIN
    IF n = 1
        THEN
            factorial := 1
        ELSE
            factorial := n * factorial (n—1)
END; (* factorial *)
```

Notes:

1   This is certainly not an efficient way of calculating factorials. It is used here only as an example.
2   The value of factorial *n* grows very quickly as *n* increases. Do not be surprised if the value exceeds `maxint` with a value of *n* as low as 7.

How the example works

To calculate factorial 5 the function is called with 5 as its parameter. During the execution of the function it causes itself to be called with 4 as its parameter. This process continues until 1 is passed as the parameter. This returns a value of 1, which is used to calculate the value for the call of `factorial` with 2 as its parameter, which supplies a value that allows the completion of the call of `factorial` with 3 as parameter and so on until the call of `factorial` with 5 as parameter can be completed.

A more practical example

To write a positive integral value in binary using the technique of repeatedly dividing by 2 and taking remainders. For example:

61 div by 2	30 rem 1
30 div by 2	15 rem 0
15 div by 2	7 rem 1
7 div by 2	3 rem 1
3 div by 2	1 rem 1
1 div by 2	0 rem 1

binary value is 111101

To do this without using a recursive technique it would be necessary to use an array to store the binary digits since the process generates them in reverse order.

The use of recursion can eliminate the need for such an array; the values will be 'stacked' by the mechanism that implements the recursion.

```
TYPE posint = 0..maxint;
PROCEDURE writebinary (n: posint);
CONST base = 2;
BEGIN
   IF n >= base
     THEN
        writebinary (n DIV base);
   write (n MOD base : 1)
END; (* writebinary *)
```

To understand this, it is useful to work through an example:

```
call writebinary (11)
     calls writebinary (11 DIV base = 5)
          calls writebinary (5 DIV base = 2)
               calls writebinary (2 DIV base = 1)
               continues by printing 1 MOD base   1
          continues by printing 2 MOD base        0
     continues by printing 5 MOD base             1
continues by printing 11 MOD base                 1
```

The denary number 11 is 1011 in binary. Note that changing the value of base allows you to write in any number system less than 10.

Mutual recursion

The recursion demonstrated so far has been direct. This means that a procedure (or function) p has contained a call of p in its own body. It sometimes happens that a procedure (or function) p calls a procedure (or function) q which contains a call to p in its body. This is called mutual or indirect recursion. (More complicated cyclic situations are possible, of course.) This causes a problem regarding the declaration of p and q.

If they are declared:

```
PROCEDURE p (x : real);
BEGIN
    (* other statements *)
    q (x) (* note *)
    (* other statements *)
END; (* p *)

PROCEDURE q (x : real);
BEGIN
    (* other statements *)
    p (x)
    (* other statements *)
END; (* q *)
```

then the call to q in the line marked (* note *) will be invalid since at that stage q has not been declared. Clearly it does not help if the order of declarations is reversed.

The problem (of a forward reference) is solved by the following construction:

```
PROCEDURE q (x : real); forward;
    (* no body at this point *)
PROCEDURE p (x : real);
BEGIN
    (* other statements *)
    q (x)
    (* other statements *)
END; (* p *)

PROCEDURE q; (* note-parameters not repeated *)
```

```
BEGIN
   (* other statements *)
   p (x)
   (*other statements *)
END; (* q *)
```

This feature does not appear in the Pascal Report but only in the User Manual. (Section 11C). `forward` is a standard word – not a reserved word. Some implementations allow the parameters (of q in this case) to be repeated, but they must match those given in the forward declaration.

Passing procedures and functions as parameters to procedures and functions

If a procedure or function is to be used as a parameter to another procedure or function then it must not have any `VAR` parameters. *Example:* procedure as parameter:

```
PROCEDURE error (code : integer);
BEGIN
   (* handle error *)
END; (* error *)
(*a*) PROCEDURE process (x : real;
                         PROCEDURE errhandler);
      BEGIN
         IF x < O THEN
               errhandler (y)
               ELSE
                  and so on
      END
      BEGIN (* main *)
            process (y, error);
            and so on
```

Example: using a function as a parameter

```
FUNCTION g (x : real) : real;
(* any function of x *)
BEGIN
      g :=
END; (* g *)
(* b *) FUNCTION integrate (FUNCTION f: real; a, b:
        real): real; (* integrate f over the range a
        to b *)
        BEGIN
        END; (* integrate *)
        to use integrate :
y : = integrate (g, 1.0, 2.0)
```

Note: many implementations do not permit the use of standard functions as parameters (including UCSD).

Standardised extensions

In the proposal for a standard Pascal by the British Standards Institute (BSI), the syntax for procedure and function parameters requires the parameters of these procedures or functions. In this form of Pascal the preceding example of a procedure as a parameter would need to be changed to:

```
PROCEDURE process (x : real; PROCEDURE errhandler
(code : integer));
```

on the line marked (* a *).
The second example would need to be changed to:

```
FUNCTION integrate (FUNCTION f (x : real) : real; a, b :
real) : real;
```

on the line marked (* b *).

Conformant arrays

See Chapter 14 for extensions allowing different sizes of array to be passed as parameters.

Exercise using recursion

9.4 The Fibonacci numbers are defined for positive integers as follows:

> fib_1 (the first Fibonacci number) is 1
> fib_2 is 1
> fib_n (the nth Fibonacci number) is $\text{fib}_{n-1} + \text{fib}_{n-2}$

Write two Pascal functions each of which accepts n as a parameter and returns the value of the nth Fibonacci number. One function should be iterative and the other recursive.

Which of your functions more closely reflects the definition of Fibonacci numbers?

Which of your functions do you think would involve the lesser computation?

Time them on your implementation if possible.

10

Top-down Programming

Design of programs

When you write fairly small and simple computer programs you probably find that you can write down the necessary statements without giving much thought to the design of the program.

However, if the task is larger, it becomes essential to undertake a considerable amount of planning before you begin writing the Pascal statements.

The traditional tool in such planning has been the flowchart but this has the disadvantage (if not used carefully) of encouraging you to be too concerned about details at an early stage.

Various other techniques are now widely used and are termed 'structured programming'. Most approaches (some of which are very rigid and detailed) fall into a category called 'top-down' techniques.

Using one such method, 'stepwise refinement', you should start planning by stating the task to be performed by your program. The next step is to divide that task into a series of smaller components. In the next step each component is broken down itself and the process continues until each component is capable of being expressed in a small number of Pascal statements.

At any given stage the components may need to be repeated or carried out conditionally. When using many other programming languages it has been conventional to use a 'pseudo' language to express this repetition or conditional use. However, the structured control statements of Pascal (WHILE, IF, CASE...) render such a pseudo-language unnecessary.

For example, consider a program that is to read a series of (whole) numbers from a file and find their total and average.

Step 1: 'find total and average of numbers on file'
Step 2: Set up counters and open file
      WHILE NOT end of file DO
        read number and update counters
      Calculate print total and average

At this point you have the option of further refining each step or, by using procedures and/or functions, you could make the above statement of the problem the basis of your main program. This 'modular' approach is definitely a great advantage when you are writing larger programs.

Whatever approach is taken, it is necessary to refine each component of the description of the problem as given in step 2. In this case, the final refinement can be to a completed Pascal program.

```
PROGRAM average (f, output);
VAR f : text;
    count, n, total : integer;
PROCEDURE setup;
BEGIN
    count := 0;
    total := 0;
    reset (f)
END; (* setup *)

PROCEDURE readandupcount;
BEGIN
        readln (f, n);
        total := total + n;
        count := count + 1
END; (* readandupcount *)

PROCEDURE calcandprint;
VAR average : real;
BEGIN
        average := total/count;
        writeln (' average is ', average)
END; (* calcandprint *)

BEGIN (* main program *)
        setup;
        WHILE NOT eof (f) DO
            readandupcount;
        calcandprint
END. (* main program *)
```

Notice that the main program is really a statement of step 2 of the refinement. Because of the small size of this example the benefits of the top-down approach do not really show up well. In larger programs, however, this approach will certainly make a program easier to read, understand and modify. When reading a program written in this style you can read through the main program to find out the overall structure of the program and then refer to the text of those procedures in the main program that you want to find out more about.

Try reading the exam results example program in this way. (It includes the use of sets which are explained later, but this is not important to the general understanding of the program.)

11

A Structured Type – the SET

The concept of a set

A set is a structured type that can be represented directly in Pascal. The syntax for manipulating sets closely follows the notation of set theory and is very easy to use.

A set is a collection of possible items, any of which may or may not be present. For example, the prime numbers less than 20 form a set of numbers.

In Pascal a set may be composed of elements of any ordinal type (that excludes real) (see Fig. 11.1). For example, a set may have

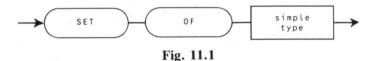

Fig. 11.1

elements that are the numbers 1 to 20. This would be declared in Pascal as:

```
TYPE onetotwenty = 1..20;
VAR numbers : SET OF onetotwenty;
    onenumber : onetotwenty;
```

Note that onenumber can contain any value between 1 and 20 inclusive, while numbers can contain any, all or none of those values.

Sets can also be composed of values of an enumeration type and examples based on this are probably easier to understand (Fig.

11.2). Set constants are formed by using square brackets [ ]. Within the brackets you can put those elements which are to be present in this set, separated by commas, in any order, or an inclusive range of values indicated by the .. symbol. The empty set is indicated by [ ].

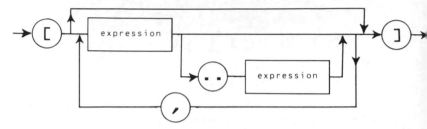

Fig. 11.2

Using sets – an example using an enumeration type

```
TYPE country = (A,   (* Austria      *)
                B,   (* Belgium      *)
                CH,  (* Switzerland  *)
                D,   (* Germany      *)
                DK,  (* Denmark      *)
                E,   (* Spain        *)
                F,   (* France       *)
                GB,  (* Great Britain *)
                GR,  (* Greece       *)
                I,   (* Italy        *)
                IRL,(* Ireland      *)
                L,   (* Luxembourg   *)
                N,   (* Norway       *)
                NL,  (* Netherlands  *)
                P,   (* Portugal     *)
                S,   (* Sweden       *) );
VAR all, eec, originaleec, benelux,
    driveonright, frenchspoken, germanspoken,
    bothspoken, usemetric : SET OF country;
```

Set constants:

```
all := [A..S]
driveonright := [A..F, L..S, GR, I]
benelux := [B, NL, L]
```

Note that the order of elements is only significant with the .. symbol.

The set union operator, +

The + operator forms the union of two sets, that is, it gives a set which has those elements that were in either or both sets. For example:

```
originaleec := benelux + [F, D, I,]
EEC := originaleec + [GB, IRL, DK, GR]
```

The set difference operator, –

The – operator forms a set that has the elements of the first set but excluding those of the second. For example:

```
usemetric := all — [GB,IRL]
```

The set intersection operator, *

The * operator gives a set that contains the elements which were in both sets. For example:

```
frenchspoken := [F, B, CH, L];
germanspoken := [D, CH, A, L];
bothspoken := frenchspoken * germanspoken;
    (*gives the value [CH,L]*)
```

Comparing sets

Sets may be compared using any of these four of the relational operators: =, < >, >=, <=:

1   = true if sets have identical elements
    For example:

```
driveonright = usemetric (true)
```

2   <> true if sets do not have identical elements. For example:

```
driveonright <> eec (true)
```

3   >= 'contains' – first set includes all elements of second. For example:

```
eec >= originaleec (true)
```

4 <= 'is contained by'
For example:

```
[F] <= frenchspoken (true)
```

An additional operator, IN, tests to see if an element is a member of a set. For example:

```
F IN frenchspoken (true)
```

Limits on cardinality of base type:

In the preceding example the base type of the set was an enumeration type (country) of 16 elements.

Because of the way in which sets are implemented in computers there is usually a limit to the cardinality of the base type of the set. In this example the cardinality was 16. Typical values of the limit are:

ICL 1900 – 48
ICL 2900 – 256
UCSD – 512
ICL Perq – 4080

Because the compiler has to deduce the base type of a set constant there is a further restriction that the ordinal value, given by ord, of the highest value in a set constant should not exceed the limit.

Sets of characters

If, for a given implementation, the limit on the cardinality of the base type of a set is not less than the number of characters in the character set of the implementation, then the useful type SET OF char may be used. For example:

```
VAR letters, digits : SET OF char;
    ch : char;
letters := ['A'..'Z'] (or letters := ['A'..'Z',
'a'..'z'] if you have lower case).
(If your implementation uses EBCDIC code : letters :=
['a'..'i', 'j'..'r', 's'..'z'].)
digits := ['0'..'9']
IF ch IN letters tests that ch is alphabetic.
```

IF ch IN letters + digits tests that ch is alphabetic or numeric.

IF ch IN ['a'..'d'] tests that ch is 'a' or 'b' or 'c' or 'd'.

Exercise

11.1   Write a Pascal program to count (separately) the following characters in a segment of text:
   - (*a*) upper-case letters
   - (*b*) lower-case letters
   - (*c*) numeric digits
   - (*d*) spaces (including ends of lines)
   - (*e*) others

Print out the total of each sort. Assume SET OF char is available.

12

Files of Type other than char

Files of any type

So far you have used files of type `text`, which means `FILE OF char` – file of characters. This is very appropriate for any file that you want to be able to type data into from keyboard or to read, since you can only conveniently read files that contain values which appear as characters.

Inside the computer, however, values are not stored as characters (unless they are of type `char` or arrays of `char`). For example, an integer with a value of 12 does not hold the characters '1' and '2' but a binary, machine representation of the number 12. Unless you have a good knowledge of the internal workings of the computer such values will not be of interest to you. Sometimes, however, you may be producing a file of data with a program and reading it with another program. It is not necessary to convert all the values to a character representation during output from the first program and back to internal representation during input to the second.

It is possible to declare files to be of almost any type and thus imply that internal representation is to be input or output directly. For example, declaring a file of type other than `char`:

```
PROGRAM example (input, output, notchars);
TYPE anything = (* any type you like *);
VAR notchars : FILE OF anything;
```

There is usually a restriction to prevent you declaring such things as:

```
FILE OF FILE OF
```

which most implementations cannot cope with.

To use such files, note that the concept of a line only pertains to files of characters. This means that readln, writeln and eoln have no meaning in this context and cannot be used. However, eof is still available. If a file is declared as:

```
VAR stressvalues : FILE OF real;
    thisvalue    : real;
```

then each value on the file will be of type real. To read a value from such a file:

```
read (filename, thisvalue)
```

or to write a value to such a file

```
write (filename, thisvalue)
```

For example:

```
read (stressvalues, thisvalue)
```

or

```
write (stressvalues, thisvalue)
```

are sometimes available (UCSD).

However, many implementations do not make read and write available except for FILE OF char. Instead you must build each operation from its (two) component statements as shown below.

Buffer variables

To understand how this works you need to know that for every file used in the program there is a buffer variable, named as filename^ e.g. stressvalues^. This buffer is of type x if the file is defined as FILE OF x, so in this example it is the real value currently in the buffer. As discussed in Chapter 4, the read operation works by transferring what is in the buffer (first value put there by reset (filename)) and then reloading the buffer.

This is how eof anticipates the physical end of a file. The equivalent of a read in lower level terms is:

```
recordname := filename ^;)* transfer from buffer to
                              named record *)
get (filename ); (* reload buffer from physical
                              file *)
```

if the buffer cannot be reloaded by get then its value is left undefined but eof (filename) becomes true. The equivalent of write is:

```
filename^:=recordname;(* transfer to buffer from
                                   named value *)
put (filename); (* transmit contents of buffer to
                                 physical file *)
```

Alternatively, you can use buffer directly as variables of the appropriate type and then inspect the buffer as in Chapter 4. Do not forget to use:

reset on files for input

and

rewrite on files for output

You may wish to create programs to read and write files where each record is a Pascal RECORD structure holding useful information. You can take advantage of the facilities for files of various types to avoid work between programs. To create a file from the keyboard:

```
PROGRAM create (input, output, stocks);
TYPE stocktype = RECORD
                 code : integer;
                 description : PACKED ARRAY
                 [1..20] OF char;
                 recordlevel : integer;
                 reorderquantity : integer;
                 current : integer
                 END; (* stocktype *)
VAR currentrec : stocktype;
    stocks     : FILE OF stocktype;
BEGIN rewrite (stocks);
    (* set information from input *)
    WITH currentrec DO
    BEGIN (* build up current record *)
        stocks ^:= currentrec;
        put (stocks);
    END; (* with *)
    writeln ('finished')
END.
```

To use the file:

```
PROGRAM useit (output, stocks);
TYPE stocktype = (* as in create *);
VAR currentrec : stocktype;
    stocks     : FILE OF stocktype;
BEGIN
    reset (stocks);
    WHILE NOT eof (stocks) DO
        BEGIN
            currentrec := stocks ^;
            get (stocks);
            (* process currentrec *)
        END
END.
```

Exercise

12.1 A file called `infile` consists of records consisting of two `real` values. A second file, called `outfile`, consists of records consisting of one `real` value.

    Write a complete program to read records from `infile` and create records for `outfile` such that the single `real` value on a record for `outfile` is the sum of the corresponding values on `infile`.

13

Dynamic Data Structures

The concept of dynamic data

So far all the variables and data structures used in your programs have been static in the sense that their existence, structure and size have all been determined at the same time that you wrote the program and, as far as the computer is concerned, at the time you compiled the program.

In fact, using the facilities of Pascal that you have met so far, all the characteristics of all variables can be determined when the program is compiled. This is not always convenient. You may already have encountered situations in programming where you would like, for example, the size of an array to be determined by the value of some variable or expression that can only be determined when the program runs and you probably overcame the difficulty by declaring the array to be as large as the maximum value you would possibly encounter. This, of course, is wasteful of space – a commodity that can be scarce on a small computer.

Certain other high-level languages (for example, Algol 68) give the ability to determine the size of arrays at runtime but Pascal offers a general-purpose approach that allows great flexibility in the creation and manipulation of variables at runtime. Such variables are called dynamic. (They are also available in Algol 68 and various other languages.)

Clearly, if real flexibility is to be achieved then the creation and manipulation of dynamic variables cannot be achieved in the same way as for normal, static variables since they are limited by what you write. Additionally, dynamic variables can come into existence (and disappear) in a way that is completely unrelated to block-structures implied by the use of procedures and functions.

Dynamic variables are created in an area of the store of the computer separate from the static variables. This area is referred to as the 'heap'. This term is used to reflect the fact that the organisation of variables in this part of the store is usually rather less ordered than that of the 'stack', where the static variables are held.

In certain implementations of Pascal the size of the heap space is limited, though usually under your control. It may be necessary for you to keep a check on how much heap space a program uses in a typical run so as to be sure of making sufficient heap available.

In UCSD Pascal the heap and stack occupy the same fixed space with the stack advancing from one end as blocks (procedures or functions) are entered and collapsing as the program leaves them. The heap advances from the other end of the fixed space under the control of Pascal statements that you will see soon, and retreats under the other control of other Pascal statements.

If insufficient fixed space is allocated then the program may fail with a message:

```
Heap and/or stack overflow
```

as the heap and stack collide.

Pointers

Reference to dynamic variables is achieved by means of pointers which are variables that hold the address (position in store) of the variables to which they point. In order to use a dynamic structure there must be at least one static pointer that can refer to it. The Pascal syntax for declaring a pointer is given in Fig. 13.1. For example, a pointer to an integer would be declared as:

```
VAR pointtointeger : ^integer;
```

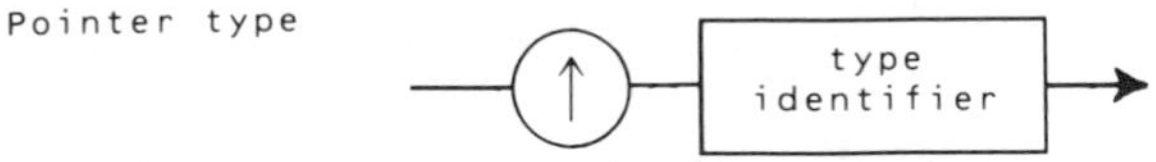

Pointer type

Fig. 13.1

(The circumflex (^) symbol – as used in this book – is a common alternative to the vertical arrow (↑), which is not always available in the computer's character set. The commercial 'at' (ⓐ) sign can also be used as an alternative.)

Pointers to integers, however, are not particularly useful. What are very useful are pointers to structures which themselves contain pointers, because this enables new parts to grow from the pointers.

Linked lists

The simplest example of a dynamic data structure is the 'linked list' in which each element (or atom) is connected to the next by a pointer. A linked list can be thought of as looking something like Fig. 13.2. Note that the only variable which is declared statically is the first position. The rest is created at runtime. Note that the data value can be of any type (including pointer type). The necessary declarations for creating a linked list as illustrated are:

```
TYPE datatype = (* any type *);
     pointer = ^ atom;
     atom = RECORD
              datavalue : datatype;
              point     :pointer
              END; (* atom *)
VAR list : pointer;
```

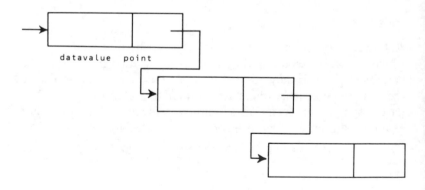

Fig. 13.2

This is the only occasion in Pascal where, of necessity, a type can

be referred to before it has been declared. (Use of `^atom`
precedes declaration of `atom`.) This is called a recursive
definition: the definition of `atom` refers to itself. Most dynamic
structures are recursively defined. This is what affords them
their great flexibility. Recursive procedures are extremely
useful in the processing of recursively-defined structures.

The pointer constant `NIL`

In the example above the only variable declared statically was
called `list`, of type `pointer` (to an atom). Like all variables in
Pascal, it has an undefined initial value, in this case it is pointing to
an undefined location in the store. There is a universal constant of
type pointer (to anything) called `NIL`. Its value can be assigned to a
pointer variable and can be tested for by means of = and <>. For
example:

```
list := NIL;
IF list = NIL THEN ...
IF list <> NIL THEN ...
```

The value `NIL` is very useful for marking the end(s) of a dynamic
structure. Pointers of the same type can be compared for equality or
inequality.

Creating dynamic variables by means of `new`

In order to give a variable such as `list` something to point to, not
just a `NIL` pointer, you use the `new` statement. For example:

```
new (list)
```

This has two effects:

1 It acquires space in the heap for a variable of the type that the
   variable in brackets (`list`) is declared to point to, that is, an
   `atom`.
2 It puts the address of the newly created `atom` into the variable
   supplied in brackets, that is `list`.

Its effect can be thought of as depicted in Fig. 13.3. Note that the
values of the components of this new `atom` are undefined.

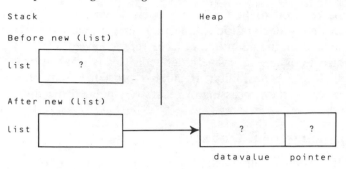

Fig. 13.3

Using pointers

If you wish to give values to this new `atom` you must do so by means of your only static pointer. If you wrote:

```
list.datavalue := datavalue
```

to give the `datavalue` part a value and:

```
list.pointer := NIL
```

to mark the (current) end of the list, then you would find a syntax error reported in your program since `list` is not a record but a `pointer` to a record.

To indicate this you must use the pointer symbol (↑, ^, or @) as follows:

```
list ^ .datavalue := datavalue;
list ^ .pointer   := NIL,
```

where `list ^` can be read as 'what `list` points to'. A further element can be added to the list by writing:

```
new (list ^ .pointer);
```

and values given to it by means of:

```
list ^ .pointer ^ .datavalue := datavalue;
```

and:

```
list ^ .pointer ^ .pointer := NIL;
```

Clearly this means of designation is tedious and limiting and the situation can be simplified by using one (or more) extra static variables to point to, for example, the current end of the list.

Disposing of dynamic variables

When dynamic variables are no longer required they need not necessarily be disposed of. However, when heap space is limited it is possible that the space used by unwanted variables could usefully be made available for the creation of new variables. There are two ways of doing this:

1 By means of the `dispose` statement (standard Pascal).
2 By means of `mark` and `release` (UCSD Pascal).

Sometimes this facility is not provided at all. Sometimes `dispose` merely makes the variable inaccessible without making its space reusable.

`dispose` (not UCSD)
The `dispose` procedure deletes elements of dynamic structures. Its parameter is the name of a pointer variable and the variable pointed to is disposed of and its space made available for future dynamic variables. Note that `dispose` does not follow pointers and must be used with care lest inaccessible variables remain (Fig. 13.4).

To dispose of an entire structure list you must arrange to dispose of each element, making sure that you never lose any vital pointers too early. The best approach usually is to find the ends and dispose backwards up to the front of the list.

`mark` and `release` (UCSD and other P-code implementations)
This technique achieves the same effect as `dispose`. You must first declare one or more (static) variables of type pointer to integer. For example:

```
VAR marker : ^ integer;
```

In the processing you can then carry out:

```
mark (marker)
```

At a later stage you can carry out:

```
release (marker)
```

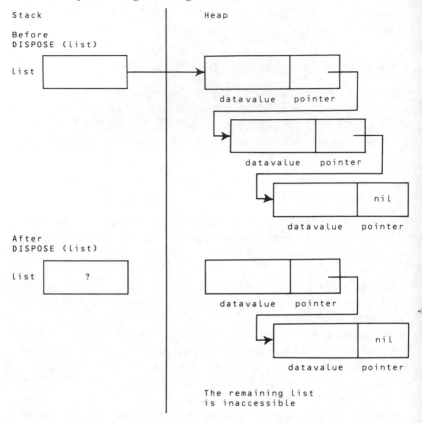

Fig. 13.4

The effect of this is to remove all dynamic variables created after
mark was carried out. It also makes their space available for reuse.
You can use several variables such as marker to achieve a nested
effect.

14

Extensions of Pascal and its Derivatives

Extensions

Although standard Pascal, as defined by Jensen and Wirth, is a very powerful language, it deliberately only contains features that can be implemented on any type of computer. Not surprisingly, many implementations of Pascal choose to include additional features that may not be capable of implementation on all machines.

This is natural and acceptable but it is desirable that such additional features should, wherever possible, be standardised.

ISO Pascal

The British Standards Institute (BSI) standard for Pascal has been accepted by the International Standards Organisation (ISO) and many implementations will now conform to this new, extended standard. The most significant extension is that of the conformant array.

In standard Pascal, when an array is to be passed as a parameter the type of the actual parameter must match the parameter declaration in all aspects. This includes the upper and lower limits of the array. Thus it is not possible to write a procedure, for example, to find the total of arrays of real values where arrays with different numbers of elements are to be supplied as parameters. It would be possible to redefine Pascal such that array bounds need not match, but this would introduce a great insecurity (the possibility of attempting to access beyond the bounds of the array).

Instead, additional syntax is included by the BSI (ISO) standard. Note also the modified syntax for procedure and function parameters (see Chapter 9). For example:

```
FUNCTION total (VAR a:ARRAY [lwb..upb:integer] OF
                                       real):real;
VAR tot : real;
    index : integer;
BEGIN
    tot := 0.0;
    FOR index := lwb TO upb DO
        tot := tot + a [index];
    total := tot
END; (* total *)
```

This function can now be applied to any array of real with integer bounds.

UCSD (University of California at San Diego)

This implementation is widely available on microcomputers and many of its extensions (and differences) have been covered in the appropriate chapters of this book. Other extensions are mainly to the implementation rather than the language and can be found in UCSD Pascal documentation. One useful extension that has not so far been mentioned is the facility for accessing files directly. This is available for files other than of type text. The records on the file can be regarded as being numbered from 0. The procedure:

```
seek (filename, integervalue)
```

causes the record with number given by integer value to be accessed by the next get or put (or read or write).

Common areas of extension

Usually the documentation of a Pascal implementation will include a list of extensions (and differences) as compared with standard Pascal. A list of common extensions follows:

1 ELSE or OTHERWISE in a CASE statement to deal with values of selector for which no constant is supplied.
2 Ability to call in procedures (subroutines) written in other

languages available on the same machine (allows use of existing libraries of procedures written in, say, FORTRAN).

3   Ability to compile procedures or groups of procedures separately from each other or the main program. This facilitates the development of very large programs. An extension of this is the *module* concept of Modula–2 or the *unit* of UCSD Pascal.

4   Ability to input and output values of enumeration types directly.

5   More flexible variable names (use lower case or underline character to aid legibility).

6   Power operator ** or ^ as in FORTRAN or BASIC.

7   Numeric constants to bases other than 10.

8   Relaxation of order of declarations (LABEL, CONST, TYPE and so on).

9   Constants defined as constant expressions calculated by compiler.

10   Error trapping routines by means of 'exceptions' (this is also a feature of Ada).

Portability

If it is important to you that your programs should work on more than one machine then it will be wise to avoid the use of implementation extensions wherever possible. This should be fairly easy, since most extensions are included for reasons of convenience rather than necessity.

Unfortunately, you will also need to take into account possible omissions or differences from standard Pascal in the implementations you are using.

Do not forget that different machines may have different character codes. (See notes on EBCDIC throughout this book.)

Languages based on Pascal

Certain extensions to Pascal are so great that they effectively turn into a new language. Such languages are usually designed to fulfil a rather different role than Pascal's. In particular, many such extensions have been directed towards the needs of real-time applications and parallel programming. The following list includes some of these major extensions to Pascal:

1   Modula–2: a derivative of Pascal designed by Niklaus Wirth (the author of Pascal) at ETH, Zurich, it is specially designed for systems programming and real-time applications.
2   Pascal-Plus: this includes extensions of Pascal for parallel processing (real-time and systems applications) by D. Bustard, Queens University, Belfast.
3   Concurrent Pascal: the use of Pascal is extended for parallel processing (real-time and systems applications) by Professor Per Brinch Hansen, University of Southern California.
4   Ada: named after Countess Ada Lovelace, assistant to Charles Babbage, inventor of early mechanical computers, this is a new high-order language commissioned by the US Department of Defense and intended for real-time (embedded) systems. This language is much larger than Pascal, although based on it, and requires powerful computer facilities.

At the time of writing the complexity of Ada, and the possible concomitant insecurities, are being vigorously debated. Its sponsorship alone, however, will imply that the language will become important.

If you wish to learn Ada then a knowledge of Pascal forms an excellent starting point.

Appendix A
Delimiter Words

Delimiter words (reserved words) (do not use as identifiers):

AND	DOWNTO	IF	OR	THEN
ARRAY	ELSE	IN	PACKED	TO
BEGIN	END	LABEL	PROCEDURE	TYPE
CASE	FILE	MOD	PROGRAM	UNTIL
CONST	FOR	NIL	RECORD	VAR
DIV	FUNCTION	NOT	REPEAT	WHILE
DO	GOTO	OF	SET	WITH

Extensions sometimes include:

OTHERWISE   VALUE

Appendix B
Standard Identifiers

Standard identifiers (do not use as identifiers):

Constants:	false, true, maxint
Types:	integer, real, boolean, char, text
Files:	input, output
Functions:	abs, arctan, chr, cos, eof, eoln, exp, ln, odd, ord, pred, round, sin, sqr, sqrt, succ, trunc
Procedures:	dispose, get, new, pack, page, put, read, readln, reset, rewrite, unpack, write, writeln
Directive:	forward

Extension (mainly UCSD)

Types:	string, interactive
Functions:	atan (in place of arctan), log, pwroften, length, pos, concat, copy
Procedures:	delete, insert, str, close, seek, mark, release

and others.

Appendix C
Collected Syntax Diagrams (BSI)

Identifier

Unsigned integer

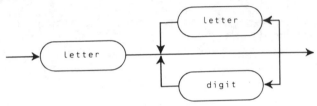

Unsigned number

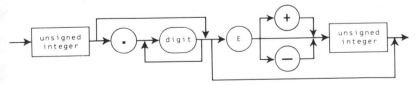

Unsigned constant

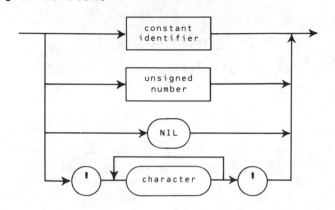

Constant

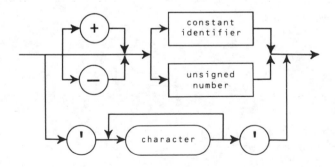

Simple type

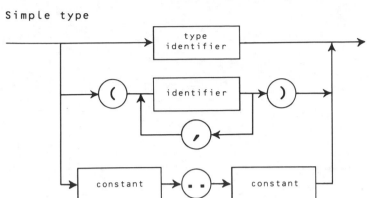

Type

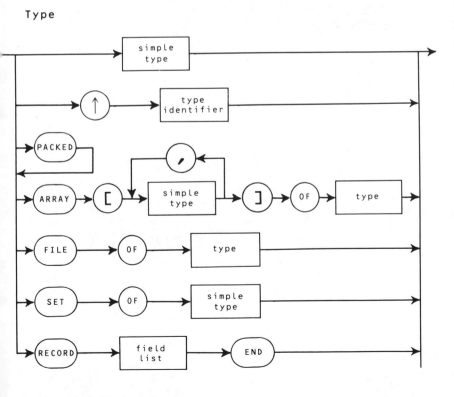

Field list

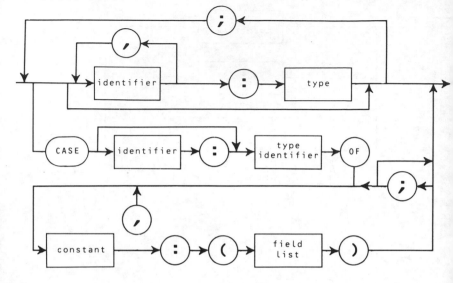

Variable

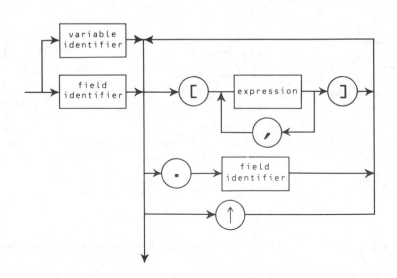

Factor

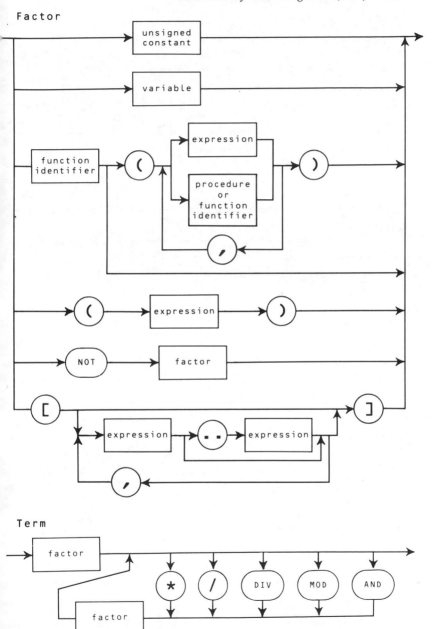

Term

Simple expression

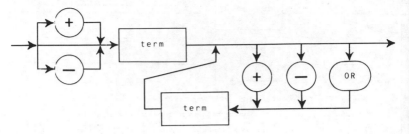

Expression

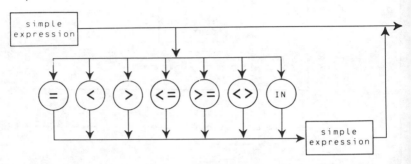

Parameter list

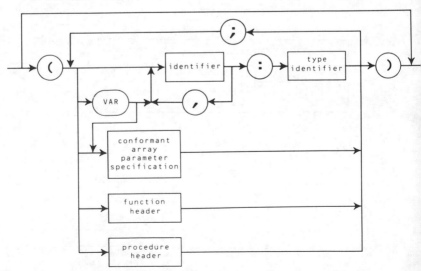

Procedure header

Function header

Conformant array parameter specification
(BSI Level 1)

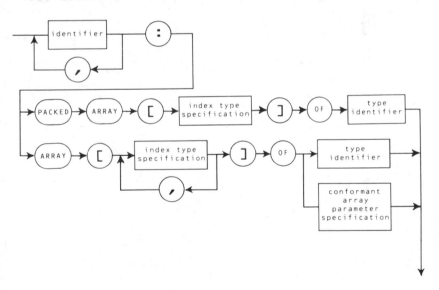

Index type specification

Statement

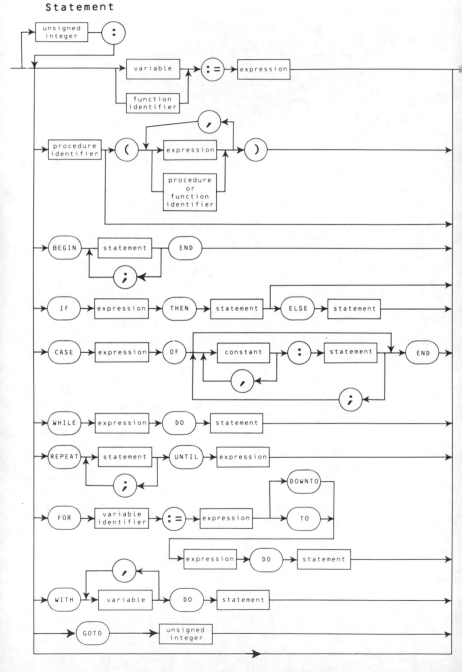

Block

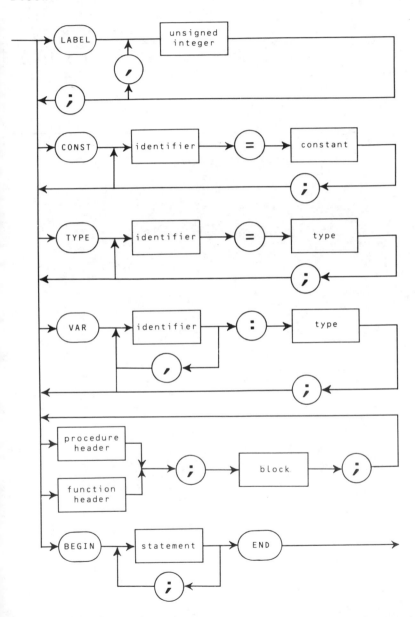

Program

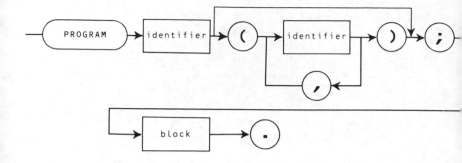

Further Reading

Pascal User Manual and Report, second edition, Kathleen Jensen and Niklaus Wirth, Springer-Verlag. (The original reference book on Pascal.)

Pascal with Style – Programming Proverbs, Henry F. Ledgard, John F. Heuras and Paul A. Nasin, Hayden Book Company Inc. (Guide to good style in Pascal.)

Algorithms + Data Structures = Programs, Niklaus Wirth, Prentice-Hall Inc. (Advanced uses of Pascal – contains concise introduction to language.)

Systematic Programming: An Introduction, Niklaus Wirth, Prentice-Hall Inc. (Highly technical – uses Pascal to illustrate points.)

Pascal: The Language and its Implementation, edited by D. W. Barron, Wiley. (Conference collection of papers on Pascal.)

The Byte Book of Pascal, edited by Blaise Liffick, McGraw-Hill. (Collection of articles on Pascal from Byte magazine – mainly for small machines.)

Programming in Modula-2, Niklaus Wirth, Springer-Verlag. (Definition of the language Modula-2 and good general-purpose text on programming.)

Specification for the Computer Programming Language Pascal, British Standards Institute, 2 Park Street, London W1A 2BS.

Solutions to Exercises

Exercise 1.1

(*a*) Valid
(*b*) Valid
(*c*) Valid
(*d*) Invalid: / not allowed
(*e*) Valid
(*f*) Invalid: reserved word
(*g*) Invalid: space not allowed
(*h*) Valid but inadvisable: standard type
(*i*) Valid but may be inadvisable in same program as `datafile1`
(*j*) Invalid: must start with letter, cannot contain −

Answers given as complete programs:

Exercise 2.1

```
PROGRAM example;
VAR mark    : integer;
    average : real;
    pass    : boolean;
    level   : char;
BEGIN
    mark := 51;
    average := 47.5;
    level := 'a'
    pass := true
END.
```

Exercise 2.2

```
PROGRAM leapyear (input, output);
(* assign true to 'leap' if year is leap,
                            otherwise false *)
VAR year : integer;
    leap : boolean;
BEGIN
    read ( year );
    leap := ( year MOD   4  = 0 ) AND
            ( year MOD 100 <> 0 ) OR
            ( year MOD 400 = 0 );
(* if year is divisible by 4 *)
(* but not by 100            *)
(* or it is divisible by 400 *)
    IF leap
        THEN
            writeln ( year, ' is a leap year ')
        ELSE
            writeln ( year, ' is not a leap year ')
END.
```

Exercise 2.3

```
PROGRAM grid (input, output);
VAR point1, point2,
    east1, east2,
    north1, north2 : integer;
    distance    : real;
BEGIN
    read (point1);
    read (point2);
    east1  := point1 DIV 10000;
    east2  := point2 DIV 10000;
    north1 := point1 MOD 10000;
    north2 := point2 MOD 10000;
    distance := sqrt (sqr(east1 - east2) +
                        sqr(north1 - north 2) );
    writeln ( ' distance is ', distance)
END.
```

Exercise 2.4

```
PROGRAM fitzgerald (input, output);
CONST c = 2.99792458e+8;
VAR   lrest,
      lnew,
      v     : real;
```

```
BEGIN
      read (lrest);
      read (v);
      lnew := lrest * sqrt
                        (1.0 - sqr (v) / sqr (c));
      writeln (lnew)
END.
```

Exercise 2.5

```
PROGRAM me29 (input, output);
CONST degtorad = 0.0174532925;
VAR elevation,
      beamrange,
      horizontal,
      angels,
      radians      : real;
BEGIN
    read (elevation, beamrange);
    radians := elevation * degtorad;
    horizontal := beamrange * cos (radians);
    angels := beamrange * sin (radians);
    writeln ('bandits at ', horizontal , ' units ');
    writeln ('angels ', angels )
END.
```

Exercise 3.1

```
PROGRAM ex3p1;
VAR hours, minutes : integer;
BEGIN
 IF hours > 12
     THEN
        hours := hours - 12
END.
```

Exercise 3.2

```
PROGRAM ex3p2;
VAR hours, minutes : integer;
    tomorrow : boolean;
BEGIN
    minutes := minutes + 30;
    IF minutes >= 60
        THEN
          BEGIN
            minutes := minutes - 60;
            hours := hours + 1
          END;
```

```
        hours := hours + 7;
        IF hours >= 24
            THEN
              BEGIN
                hours := hours - 24;
                tomorrow := true
              END
            ELSE
              tomorrow := false
END.
```

Exercise 3.3

```
PROGRAM ex3p3;
VAR power : integer;
BEGIN
    power := 1;
    REPEAT
        power := power * 2;
        write (power)
    UNTIL power > 1000
END.
```

Exercise 4.1

```
PROGRAM corrected ( input,output );
(* finds average of whole numbers
    - one per line              *)
VAR total,
    count,
    n         : integer;
    average : real;
BEGIN
    total:= 0;
    count:= 0;
    WHILE NOT eof DO
        BEGIN
            readln ( n );
            total := total + n;
            count := count + 1
        END;
    IF count = 0
        THEN
            writeln ( 'no numbers read' )
        ELSE
            writeln ( 'average is ', total/count )
END.
```

Exercise 5.1

```
TYPE yearincentury = 1900 .. 1999;
```

Exercise 5.2

```
PROGRAM  terms;
    TYPE  term = (michaelmas,lent,summer);
VAR       thisterm,nextterm : term;
BEGIN     ( * assume value given to this term * )
    IF thisterm = summer
      THEN
        nextterm := michaelmas
      ELSE
        nextterm := succ (thisterm)
END.
```

Exercise 6.1

```
PROGRAM launch ( output );
VAR    countdown : integer;
BEGIN
    FOR countdown := 10 DOWNTO 1 DO
        writeln( countdown )
END.
```

Exercise 6.2

```
PROGRAM table ( output );
CONST factor  = 261.378;
      hundred = 100.0;
VAR   x,
      y    : real;
      step : integer;
BEGIN
    FOR step := 100 TO 300 DO
        BEGIN
        x := step / hundred;
        y := factor * sqrt ( 1.0 + sqr(x));
        writeln ( x, y )
        END
END.
```

Exercise 6.3

```
PROGRAM nicerquad ( input, output );
(* sort of roots equation ax2 + bx + c has *)
```

```
CONST eps = 1.0e-10;
(* tolerance - absolute values smaller than this are
                         treated as zero        *)
VAR   a,
      b,
      c,
      discr : real;
      count : integer;
BEGIN (*nicerquad *)
   count := 0;
   WHILE NOT eof DO
      BEGIN        (* loop through file *)
         readln (a,b,c);
         write  (a,b,c);
         count := count + 1;
         IF abs ( a ) < eps
            THEN
               IF abs ( b ) < eps
                  THEN
                     writeln (' no solution ')
                  ELSE
                     writeln (' single root ')
            ELSE
               BEGIN   (* roots are quadratic *)
                  discr := sqr(b) - 4.0*a*c;
                  IF discr > eps
                     THEN
                        writeln (' real roots ')
                     ELSE
                        IF discr < -eps
                           THEN
                              writeln
                            (' complex roots ')
                           ELSE
                              writeln
                            (' coincident roots ')
               END (* roots are quadratic *)
      END;     (* loop through file *)
   writeln (' no. of records processed = ', count )
END.
```

Exercise 6.4

```
PROGRAM mensa;
VAR   daysinmonth : 1..31;
      month       : ( jan,feb,mar,apr,may,june,
                      jul,aug,sep,oct,nov,dec);
      leap        : boolean;
BEGIN
   (* values given to 'month' and 'leap' *)
```

```
        CASE month OF
            jan,mar,may,jul,
            aug,oct,dec        :   daysinmonth := 31;
            apr,jun,sep,nov    :   daysinmonth := 30;
            feb                :   IF leap THEN
                                           daysinmonth := 29
                                   ELSE
                                           daysinmonth := 28
        END (* of case *)
END.
```

Exercise 7.1

```
PROGRAM   aboveaverage ( input, output );
CONST arraylimit = 100;
VAR   x,
      average,
      total    : real;
      count ,
      i        : integer;
      values   : ARRAY [1..arraylimit] OF real;
BEGIN
    count := 0;
    total := 0.0;
    WHILE NOT eof AND ( count < arraylimit ) DO
        BEGIN
            readln ( x );
            count := count + 1;
            total  := total + x;
            values [ count ] := x
        END;
    IF count <> 0
        THEN
          BEGIN
            average := total / count;
            FOR i := 1 TO count DO
                IF values [ i ] > average
                    THEN
                        writeln ( values [ i ] )
          END
        ELSE
          writeln ('no values given')
END.
```

Exercise 7.2

```
PROGRAM matrices (input, output);
CONST   rowlim = 3;
        collim = 5;
```

```
TYPE      matrix = ARRAY [1..rowlim] OF
                              ARRAY[1..collim] OF real;
(* or    ARRAY [1..rowlim, 1..collim ] OF real; *)
VAR      a, b, c : matrix;
         row     : 1..rowlim;
         col     : 1..collim;
BEGIN
   (* assuming values given to a and b *)
   FOR row:= 1 TO rowlim DO
      FOR col:=1 TO collim DO
         c[row,col] := a[row,col] + b[row,col]
END.
```

Exercise 7.3

```
PROGRAM exam (input, output);
CONST passmark = 40;
VAR    mark    : integer;
       pass    : ARRAY [boolean] OF integer;
       success : boolean;
BEGIN
   pass [ true ]  := 0;        (* set both elements
                              ( true and false ) *)
   pass [ false ] := 0;                 (* to zero *)
   WHILE NOT eof DO
      BEGIN
         readln ( mark );
         success := mark >= passmark;
         (* success will be true if candidate has
                      passed, otherwise false *)
         pass [ success ] := pass [ success ] + 1
      END;
   writeln ('total passes ', pass [ true ]  );
   writeln ('total fails  ', pass [ false ] )
END.
```

Exercise 7.4

```
PROGRAM frequencies (input, output);
TYPE   alfachar = 'a'..'z';
VAR    ch : char;
       index: alfachar;
       table: ARRAY [alfachar] OF integer;
BEGIN
   FOR index := 'a' TO 'z' DO table[index]:= 0;
   WHILE NOT eof DO
   BEGIN
      read(ch);
```

```
        IF (ch >= 'a') AND (ch <= 'z')
           THEN table[ch]:= table[ch] + 1
     END;
     FOR index:='a' TO 'z' DO
        writeln ( index,' occurs ',
                          table[index],' times ')
  END.
```

Exercise 8.1

```
PROGRAM types (input,output);
CONST namelength = 10;
TYPE subscript = 1 .. namelength;
     month      = ( jan, feb, mar, apr, may, jun,
                    jul, aug, sep, oct, nov, dec );
     day        = 1 .. 31;
     date       = RECORD
                     d : day;
                     m : month;
                     y : integer
                  END;
     person     = RECORD
                     name : PACKED ARRAY
                            [ subscript ] OF char;
                     birth: date;
                     death: date
                  END;
VAR  greatman : person;
BEGIN
   WITH greatman DO
   BEGIN
     name:='pascal    ';
     WITH birth DO
     BEGIN
        d:= 19; m:= jun; y:=1623
     END;
     WITH death DO
     BEGIN
        d:= 19; m:=aug; y:=1662
     END
   END;

                (* a l t e r n a t i v e l y *)

   greatman.name    := 'pascal    ';
   greatman.birth.d := 19;
   greatman.birth.m := jun;
   greatman.birth.y := 1623;
   greatman.death.d := 19;
   greatman.death.m := aug;
   greatman.death.y := 1662
END.
```

Exercise 8.2

```
PROGRAM students ( input, output, studentfile );
TYPE   code = PACKED ARRAY [ 1 .. 5 ] OF char;
       line = PACKED ARRAY [ 1 .. 25] OF char;
       studentrecord = RECORD
              name   : line;
              job    : line;
              CASE staff : boolean OF
                  true : (  dept         : code;
                            location     : code;
                            chargecode : code);
                  false: (  manager      : line;
                            companyname: line;
                            address      :
                              ARRAY[1..3] OF line)
                    END; (* record *)
VAR studentfile : FILE OF studentrecord;
BEGIN
(* dummy main program *)
END.
```

Exercise 9.1

```
PROGRAM surrex9p1;
TYPE   fieldtype = PACKED ARRAY [1 .. 10] OF char;
FUNCTION alphabetic ( field : fieldtype ) :
                                        boolean;
    CONST space = ' ';
    VAR   index : 0..10;
          ok    : boolean;
    FUNCTION alphachar ( ch : CHAR ) : boolean;
    BEGIN
        (* the following division of the range 'a' to
           'z' is only necessary on machines using the
           e.b.c.d.i.c. character set.
           this program will work for other character
           sets. *)
        alphachar := (ch >= 'a') AND (ch <= 'i') OR
                     (ch >= 'j') AND (ch <= 'r') OR
                     (ch >= 's') AND (ch <= 'z') OR
                     (ch = space )
    END; (* of alphachar *)
    BEGIN
        index := 0;
        REPEAT
           index := index + 1;
           ok := alphachar ( field [ index ] )
        UNTIL ( index = 10 ) OR NOT ok;
        alphabetic := ok
```

```
      END; (* alphabetic *)
   BEGIN
   (* dummy main program *)
   END.
```

Exercise 9.2

```
   PROGRAM surrex9p2;
   FUNCTION areaofcircle ( radius : real) : real;
      CONST pi = 3.1415926536;
      BEGIN
         areaofcircle := pi * sqr( radius )
      END; (* areaofcircle *)
   BEGIN
      (*dummy main program *)
   END.
```

Exercise 9.3

```
   PROGRAM surrex9p3;
   PROCEDURE areaandcirc ( radius : real;
                           VAR area, circum : real ):
      CONST pi = 3.1415926536;
      BEGIN
         area   := pi * sqr(radius);
         circum := 2.0 * pi * radius
      END; (* areaandcirc *)
   BEGIN
   (* dummy main program *)
   END.
```

Exercise 9.4

```
   PROGRAM test ( input, output );
   TYPE posint = 1 .. maxint;
   FUNCTION iterfib ( n : posint ) : posint;
                            (* iterative solution *)
   VAR fib1,
       fib2,
       i,
       swap : posint;
   BEGIN
      fib1 := 1;
      fib2 := 1;
      IF n < 3
         THEN
            iterfib := 1
         ELSE
```

```
    BEGIN
       FOR i := 3 TO n DO
           BEGIN
               swap:= fib2;
               fib2:= fib2 + fib1;
               fib 1:= swap
           END;
       iterfib:= fib2
    END
END; (* of iterfib *)

FUNCTION recufib ( n : posint ) : posint;
                          (* recursive solution *)
BEGIN
   IF n < 3
       THEN
           recufib := 1
       ELSE
           recufib := recufib ( n—1 ) +
                      recufib ( n—2 )
END; (* of recufib *)
BEGIN
(* dummy main program *)
END.
```

Exercise 11.1

```
PROGRAM CharSets ( input, output );
(* Uses SETs OF char to count types of characters in a
file. Counts ends of lines as spaces *)
CONST space = ' ';
VAR   uppers,
      lowers,
      numerics,
      spaces,
      others : 0 .. maxint;
      ch     : char;
BEGIN
   uppers := 0;
   lowers := 0;
   numerics := 0;
   spaces := 0;
   others := 0;
   WHILE NOT eof DO
       BEGIN
           read ( ch );
           IF ch IN [ 'A' .. 'Z' ]
               THEN
                   uppers := uppers + 1
               ELSE
```

```
                         IF ch IN [ 'a' .. 'z' ]
                             THEN
                                 lowers := lowers + 1
                             ELSE
                                 IF ch IN [ '0' .. '9' ]
                                 THEN
                                     numerics := numerics + 1
                                 ELSE
                                     IF ch = space
                                     THEN
                                         spaces := spaces + 1
                                     ELSE
                                         others := others + 1
        END;
     writeln
     (' uppers lowers numerics spaces others ' );
     writeln
     ( uppers, lowers, numerics, spaces, others )
END.
```

Exercise 12.1

```
PROGRAM nontextfiles
                ( input, output, infile, outfile );
TYPE   intype = RECORD
                    x,
                    y : real
                END;
VAR  infile  : FILE OF intype;
     inrec   : intype;
     outfile : FILE OF real;
     outval  : real;
BEGIN
    reset ( infile );
    rewrite ( outfile );
    WHILE NOT eof ( infile ) DO
        BEGIN
            inrec := infile^;
            get(infile);
            outval   := inrec.x + inrec.y;
            outfile^ := outval;
            put (outfile)
        END
END.
```

Example Programs

The following example programs should work on any 'standard' implementation of Pascal. They are included in the belief that a great deal can be learnt about programming in Pascal by studying Pascal programs. Some of the programs are referred to in the text, and they are graded as suitable for study after after reading up to (and including):

Chapter 4:
1   FirstExample
2   BigAndSmall
3   vowel
4   Helicopter
5   Jetlag
6   keypress

Chapter 9:
7   daysinterval
8   morse
9   truthtabs
10 printcalendars
11 anagram
12 fogindex

Chapter 11:
13 down
14 alfa
15 Soundex
16 CapRes
17 Exam

Chapter 13:
18 treesort

```
(* EXAMPLE PROGRAM 1 *)
(* This is a comment:
   First example Pascal program
   Note: Pascal compilers normally accept both upper case and lower case,
         treating them as equivalent.
         In this example Pascal delimiter words appear in upper case.
   End of comment *)

PROGRAM FirstExample ( input, output );
{ This is a comment too:
  Program to read pairs of whole numbers and print out larger of pair on file
  'output'.
  Continues until end of file 'input'.}

{ D e c l a r a t i o n s }
CONST endmessage = 'Program FirstExample finished. ';
VAR first, second : integer;

{ S t a t e m e n t s }
BEGIN
  WHILE NOT eof DO
    BEGIN
      read ( first, second );
      writeln ( ' first is ', first, ' second is ', second );
      write ( ' larger is ' );
      IF first > second
        THEN
          write ( first )
        ELSE
          write ( second );
      writeln;                { terminate line }
      writeln;                { blank line }
      readln                  { get new line of input }
    END; { of WHILE loop }
  writeln;
  writeln ( endmessage )
```

```
(* EXAMPLE PROGRAM 2 *)
PROGRAM BigAndSmall ( input, output );
(* To find largest, smallest and average of a series of numbers ( real )
   read from input *)

CONST terminator = '*';    (* type this to finish *)
VAR   number, largest, smallest, total : real;
      count : integer;

BEGIN
   IF eof OR (input ^ = terminator)
      THEN
         writeln ('Empty File!')
      ELSE
         BEGIN
            count := 0;
            total := 0. 0;
            read ( number );
            writeln ( number : 25 : 10 );
            count := count + 1;
            total := total + number;
            largest := number;
            smallest := number;
            readln;
            WHILE ( input^ <> terminator ) AND NOT eof DO
               BEGIN
                  read ( number );
                  writeln ( number : 25 : 10 );
                  IF number > largest
                     THEN
                        largest := number
                     ELSE
                        IF number < smallest
                           THEN
```

Example Program 2 cont.

```
                smallest := number;
                count := count + 1;
                total := total + number;
        readln
    END; (* WHILE *)
    writeln (' Count =      ', count          : 25 );
    writeln (' Largest =    ', largest        : 25 : 10 );
    writeln (' Smallest =   ', smallest       : 25 : 10 );
    writeln (' Average =    ', total / number : 25 : 10)
    END (* ELSE *)
END. (* BigAndSmall *)


(* EXAMPLE PROGRAM 3 *)
PROGRAM vowel ( input, output );
(* Count vowels in a piece of text.
   Then print totals and as percentages of
   total ( non-space ) characters *)

CONST space = ' ';
VAR   Acount,
      Ecount,
      Icount,
      Ocount,
      Ucount,
      total : integer;
      ch    : char;

BEGIN
    Acount := 0;
    Ecount := 0;
```

```
Icount := 0;
Ocount := 0;
Ucount := 0;
total  := 0;
WHILE NOT eof DO
     BEGIN
       read ( ch );
       IF( ch = 'A' ) OR ( ch = 'a' )
          THEN
             Acount := Acount + 1
          ELSE IF ( ch = 'E' ) OR ( ch = 'e' )
             THEN
                Ecount := Ecount + 1
             ELSE
                IF ( ch = 'I' ) OR ( ch = 'i' )
                   THEN
                      Icount := Icount + 1
                   ELSE
                      IF ( ch = 'O' ) OR ( ch = 'o' )
                         THEN
                            Ocount := Ocount + 1
                         ELSE
                            IF ( ch = 'U' ) OR ( ch = 'u' )
                               THEN
                                  Ucount := Ucount + 1;

       IF ch <> space
          THEN
             total := total + 1
     END, (* of file *)
writeln ('numbers of : A''s, E''s, I''s, O''s, U''s ' );
writeln; (* blank line *)
```

Example Program 3 cont.

```
      write   ('                          ');
      writeln ( '  Acount :',  7,
                '  Ecount :',  7,
                '  Icount :',  7,
                '  Ocount :',  7,
                '  Ucount :',  7 );

      write   ('Percentages ',         );
      writeln ( Acount / total * 100 : 7 : 2,
                Ecount / total * 100 : 7 : 2,
                Icount / total * 100 : 7 : 2,
                Ocount / total * 100 : 7 : 2,
                Ucount / total * 100 : 7 : 2 )

END. (* vowel *)


(* EXAMPLE PROGRAM 4 *)
PROGRAM Helicopter ( input, output );
(* Find difference between two points on a map given as
   six-digit grid references to determine whether target points
   are within range of a personal helicopter.
   BEWARE: There may be difficulties synchronizing input and output *)

CONST MinRange =  2;         (* kms *)
      MaxRange = 40;         (* kms *)
      KmsToMiles = 0.624;

VAR   BaseX,
      BaseY,
      TargetX,
      TargetY : integer;
      range   : real;
```

```
BEGIN  response : char;
  writeln; (* blank line *)
  writeln (' TYPE COORDINATES OF BASE, UNITS 100 METRES ');
  read ( BaseX, BaseY );
  REPEAT
    writeln (' TYPE COORDINATES OF TARGET, UNITS 100 METRES ');
    readln;
    read ( TargetX, TargetY );
    range := sqrt ( sqr ( TargetX — BaseX ) / 10 +
                    sqr ( TargetY — BaseY ) / 10 );
    writeln; (* blank line *)
    writeln (' RANGE IS ', range : 7 : 2, ' KMS ' );
    writeln (' ', range * KmsToMiles : 7 : 2, ' MILES ' );
    writeln; (* blank line *)
    IF range < MinRange
    THEN
        writeln ('TOO CLOSE — WALK!')
    ELSE
      IF range > MaxRange
      THEN
        writeln ('TOO FAR — USE THE JET!');

    REPEAT
      writeln; (* blank line *)
      writeln ('DO YOU WANT TO TRY SOME MORE?');
      writeln ('TYPE Y FOR YES — N FOR NO');
      readln;
      read ( response )
    UNTIL ( response = 'Y' ) OR
          ( response = 'N' ) OR
          ( response = 'y' ) OR
          ( response = 'n' )
```

Example Program 4 cont.

```
UNTIL ( response = 'N' ) OR
      ( response = 'n' );
    writeln; (* blank line *)
    writeln ('END OF PROGRAM')
END. (* Helicopter *)


(* EXAMPLE PROGRAM 5 *)
PROGRAM Jetlag ( input, output );
(* To find the rest time needed to recover from "jet Lag"
   after a flight.
   Uses Buley's formula :
   round-up-to-half-day ( T / 2 + (Z-4) + depcoef + arrcoef) / 10 days
   where T  is duration of flight in hours
         Z  is number of time zones crossed—ignore term if Z <= 4
         depcoef,
         arrcoef are departure and arrival coefficients as given below :
         time         depcoef      arrcoef
    01:00 — 07:59         3            3
    08:00 — 11:59         0            4
    12:00 — 17:59         1            2
    18:00 — 21:59         3            0
    22:00 — 00:59         4            1 *)

CONST durmax              = 40;      (* maximum duration *)
VAR   dephours, depmins,             (* departure time — local *)
      arrhours, arrmins,             (* arrival time — local *)
      durhours, durmins,             (* duration of flight *)
      depcoef,
```

```
        arrcoef,
        zones,
        Zminus4
        duration,        : integer;
        d,
        restdays         : real;
        skipcolon        : char;
BEGIN
(* input expected in form :
        departure time arrival time duration zones crossed
        for example :
        18:00           8:00        9:00        5
*)
REPEAT
    read ( dephours, skipcolon, depmins,
           arrhours, skipcolon, arrmins,
           durhours, skipcolon, durmins,
           zones )
UNTIL
    ( dephours  >= 0 ) AND ( dephours < 24 ) AND
    ( arrhours  >= 0 ) AND ( arrhours < 24 ) AND
    ( durhours  >= 0 ) AND ( durhours < durmax ) AND
    ( depmins   >= 0 ) AND ( depmins  < 60 ) AND
    ( arrmins   >= 0 ) AND ( arrmins  < 60 ) AND
    ( durmins   >= 0 ) AND ( durmins  < 60 ) AND
    ( zones     >= 0 ) AND ( zones    < 24 );
    (* This is a good place to use a function *)
IF zones > 4
    THEN
        Zminus4 := zones - 4
    ELSE
        Zminus4 := 0;
```

Example Program 5 cont.

```
  CASE dephours OF
    1,  2,  3,  4,  5,  6,  7  : depcoef := 3;
    8,  9, 10, 11               : depcoef := 0;
   12, 13, 14, 15, 16, 17      : depcoef := 1;
   18, 19, 20, 21              : depcoef := 3;
   22, 23, 0                   : depcoef := 4
  END; (* case *)
  CASE arrhours OF
    1,  2,  3,  4,  5,  6,  7  : arrcoef := 3;
    8,  9, 10, 11               : arrcoef := 4;
   12, 13, 14, 15, 16, 17      : arrcoef := 2;
   18, 19, 20, 21              : arrcoef := 0;
   22, 23, 0                   : arrcoef := 1
  END; (* case *)
  duration := durhours + ( durmins / 60 );
  d := ( duration / 2 + zminus4 + depcoef + arrcoef ) / 10;
  restdays := round ( d * 2 + 0.5 ) / 2;
  writeln('Rest days needed : ', restdays : 5 : 1 )
END. (* Jetlag *)


(* EXAMPLE PROGRAM 6 *)
PROGRAM keypress ( input, output );
(* Counts key depressions necessary to punch a file *)

CONST space = ' ';
      printon = true;
VAR   numlines,
      numchars,
      charsonline,
```

```
            charssofar,
            charssquared      : integer;
            mean,
            sigma             : real;
            ch                : char;
BEGIN
      numlines  :=0;
      numchars  :=0;
      charssquared :=0;
      WHILE NOT eof DO
      BEGIN
            numlines := numlines + 1;
            charsonline := 0;
            charssofar := 0;
            WHILE NOT eoln DO
            BEGIN
                  read ( ch );
                  IF printon
                  THEN
                        write ( ch );
                  charssofar := charssofar + 1;
                  IF ch <> space
                  THEN
                        charsonline := charssofar
            END;
      IF printon
      THEN
            writeln;
      readln;
      numchars:= numchars + charsonline;
      charssquared := charssquared + sqr(charsonline)
END; (* of through the file *)
```

Example Program 6 cont.

```
    writeln ('       summary of characters on file ');
    mean := numchars / numlines;
    sigma := sqrt( charssquared / numlines - sqr (mean) );
    writeln(' number of lines on file:        ', numlines : 3 );
    writeln(' number of characters on file :  ', numchars : 3 );
    writeln(' mean characters on line :       ', mean  : 8 : 3 );
    writeln(' standard deviation of mean
    characters per line :                     ', sigma : 8 : 3 )
    END. (* keypress *)


(* EXAMPLE PROGRAM 7 *)
PROGRAM daysinterval ( input, output );
(* Testing function 'daysbetween'
   which finds number of days between
   two dates *)

CONST earliestyear = 1752;     (* calendar changed in that year in U.K. *)
TYPE  monthtype = ( jan, feb, mar, apr, may, jun,
                    jul, aug, sep, oct, nov, dec );

      uncheckeddate
                = RECORD
                    day,
                    month,
                    year : integer
                  END; (* uncheckeddate *)

      date      = RECORD
                    day : 1 .. 31;
                    month : monthtype;
                    year : integer
                  END; (* date *)
```

```
VAR   first,
      second      : uncheckeddate;
      d1,
      d2          date;
FUNCTION leap ( year : integer ) : boolean;
BEGIN
   leap := (( year MOD 4 = 0) AND
           ( year MOD 100 <> 0 )) OR
           ( year MOD 400 = 0)
END; (* leap *)
FUNCTION daysbetween ( first,   (* and *)
                       second : date ) : integer;
VAR   totaldays : ARRAY [ monthtype ] OF 0 .. 366;
      FUNCTION daysfromstart ( this : date ) : integer;
(* count days to this date from arbitrary starting point *)
      VAR days : integer;
      BEGIN (* daysfromstart *)
         WITH this DO
         BEGIN
            days := year * 365 + year DIV 4
                  - year DIV 100 + year DIV 400
                  + totaldays [ month ]
                  + day;
            IF ( month >= mar ) AND leap ( year )
            THEN
               daysfromstart := days
            ELSE
               daysfromstart := days - 1
         END  (* with this *)
      END; (* daysfromstart *)
BEGIN (* daysbetween *)
   totaldays[jan]:= 0; totaldays[feb]:= 31; totaldays[mar]:= 59;
```

Example Program 7 cont.

```
    totaldays[apr]:=  90; totaldays[may]:=120; totaldays[jun]:=151;
    totaldays[jul]:=181; totaldays[aug]:=212; totaldays[sep]:=243;
    totaldays[oct]:=273; totaldays[nov]:=304; totaldays[dec]:=334;
    daysbetween := daysfromstart ( second ) - daysfromstart ( first )
END; (* daysbetween *)

PROCEDURE getdate ( VAR this : uncheckeddate );
(* obtains date from keyboard in form 30/10/1981 *)
VAR skip : char;
BEGIN
    WITH this DO
        BEGIN
            read ( day );
            read ( skip );              (* ignore separator *)
            read ( month );
            read ( skip );              (* ignore separator *)
            read ( year )
        END
END; (* getdate *)
FUNCTION valid ( check : uncheckeddate ) : boolean;
VAR bad : boolean;
BEGIN
    WITH check DO
        BEGIN
            bad := ( year <= earliestyear ) OR
                   ( month < 1 ) OR ( month > 12 ) OR
                   ( day < 1 ) OR ( day > 31 );
            IF NOT bad
            THEN
                CASE month OF
                1,3,5,7,8,10,12 : (* do nothing *);
```

```
              4,6,9,11  : bad := day > 30;
              2         : IF leap ( year )
                          THEN
                            bad := day > 29
                          ELSE
                            bad := day > 28
        END; (* with *)      END (* case *)
        valid := NOT bad
  END; (* valid *)

  PROCEDURE transform ( raw : uncheckeddate;
                        VAR out : date       );

  VAR m : monthtype;
      i : 2 .. 12;
  BEGIN
    out.year := raw.year;
    out.day := raw.day;
    m := jan;
    FOR i := 2 TO raw.month DO
      m := succ ( m );
    out.month := m
  END; (* transform *)
  BEGIN (* main program *)
    getdate ( first );
    WHILE NOT valid ( first ) DO
      BEGIN
        writeln ( 'date not valid — try again' );
        readln;
        getdate ( first )
      END;
    getdate ( second );
```

Example Program 7 cont.

```
WHILE NOT valid ( second ) DO
    BEGIN
        writeln (' date not valid — try again ');
        readln;
        getdate ( second )
    END;
writeln;
transform ( first, d1 );
transform ( second, d2 );
writeln(' elapsed days = ', daysbetween ( d1, d2 ))
END. (* day *)


(* EXAMPLE PROGRAM 8 *)
PROGRAM morse ( datafile, output );
(* Reads plain text from datafile and
   puts morse equivalent to output *)
CONST linewidth = 80;      (* width of output line *)
      codewidth = 5;       (* size of longest morse pattern *)
      space = '-';
      codegap = 2;         (* gap between morse codes *)
      wordgap = 3;         (* gap between words *)
TYPE linepos = 1 .. linewidth;
     widthtype = 1 .. codewidth;
     morsestring = PACKED ARRAY [ widthtype ] OF char;
     morseequiv = RECORD
                      width : widthtype;
                      value : morsestring
                  END; (* morseequiv *)
```

```pascal
VAR   table     = ARRAY [ char ] OF morseequiv;
      ch        = char;
      datafile  : text;
      pos       : 0 .. maxint;        (* not negative *)
      currmorse : morseequiv;

PROCEDURE initialise;
PROCEDURE setup ( (* using *) ch : char;
                              l : widthtype;
                              val: morsestring );

BEGIN (* setup *)
  WITH table [ ch ] DO
    BEGIN
      width := l;
      value := val
    END (* with *)
END; (* setup *)
BEGIN (* initialise *)
setup('A',2,'.-'     );  setup('B',4,'-...'   );  setup('C',4,'-.-.'  );
setup('D',3,'-..'    );  setup('E',1,'.'      );  setup('F',4,'..-.'  );
setup('G',3,'--.'    );  setup('H',4,'....'   );  setup('I',2,'..'    );
setup('J',4,'.---'   );  setup('K',3,'-.-'    );  setup('L',4,'.-..'  );
setup('M',2,'--'     );  setup('N',2,'-.'     );  setup('O',3,'---'   );
setup('P',4,'.--.'   );  setup('Q',4,'--.-'   );  setup('R',3,'.-.'   );
setup('S',3,'...'    );  setup('T',1,'-'      );  setup('U',3,'..-'   );
setup('V',4,'...-'   );  setup('W',3,'.--'    );  setup('X',4,'-..-'  );
setup('Y',4,'-.--'   );  setup('Z',4,'--..'   );
setup('0',5,'-----'  );  setup('1',5,'.----'  );  setup('2',5,'..---' );
setup('3',5,'...--'  );  setup('4',5,'....-'  );  setup('5',5,'.....' );
setup('6',5,'-....'  );  setup('7',5,'--...'  );  setup('8',5,'---..' );
setup('9',5,'----.'  );
pos := 1;
reset ( datafile )
```

Example Program 8 cont.

```
END; (* initialise *)

PROCEDURE lookup ( (* using *) VAR ch   : char;
                    (* returning *) VAR equiv : morseequiv );

BEGIN (* lookup *)
  WITH equiv DO
    BEGIN
      IF ch = space
        THEN
          BEGIN
            width := wordgap;
            value := ' '
          END
        ELSE
          IF ( ch >= 'A' ) AND ( ch <= 'I' ) OR
             ( ch >= 'J' ) AND ( ch <= 'R' ) OR
             ( ch >= 'S' ) AND ( ch <= 'Z' ) OR
             ( ch >= '0' ) AND ( ch <= '9' )
                                 (* character is acceptable *)
            THEN
              equiv := table [ ch ]
            ELSE
              BEGIN (* not recognised *)
                width := 1;
                value := '?'
              END
    END (* with *)
END; (* lookup *)

PROCEDURE checkline ( (* using *) thislength : widthtype );
BEGIN (* checkline *)
  IF pos + thislength > linewidth
    THEN
```

```
                  BEGIN (* not enough room on this line *)
                      writeln;
                      pos := 1
                  END
        ELSE
            pos := pos + thislength
END; (* checkline *)

PROCEDURE putgap ;
(* puts gaps between codes *)
BEGIN
    IF pos + codegap <= linewidth
    THEN
        BEGIN
            write ( space : codegap );
            pos := pos + codegap
        END
END; (* putgap *)
BEGIN (* morse *)
    initialise;
    WHILE NOT eof ( datafile ) DO
        BEGIN
            read ( (* from *) datafile,
                   (* returning *) ch );
            lookup ( (* using *) ch,
                     (* returning *) currmorse );
            WITH currmorse DO
                BEGIN
                    checkline ( (* using *) width );
                    write ( value : width )
                END; (* with *)
            putgap
        END; (* while *)
    writeln
END. (* morse *)
```

```
(* EXAMPLE PROGRAM 9 *)
PROGRAM truthtabs ( output );
(* prints truth tables for all boolean relationships*)

TYPE relation = ( lt, le, eq, ge, gt, ne );
     boolarray = ARRAY [ boolean, boolean ] OF boolean;
VAR rel : relation;
    tt  : boolarray;

PROCEDURE buildtable ( VAR t : boolarray;
                           rel : relation );

VAR  a, b : boolean;
BEGIN
  FOR a := false TO true DO
    FOR b := false TO true DO
      CASE rel OF
        lt : t [ a, b ] := a <  b;
        le : t [ a, b ] := a <= b;
        eq : t [ a, b ] := a =  b;
        ge : t [ a, b ] := a >= b;
        gt : t [ a, b ] := a >  b;
        ne : t [ a, b ] := a <> b
      END (* case *)
END; (* buildtable *)

PROCEDURE writebool ( x : boolean;
                      w : integer );

BEGIN
  IF x
    THEN
      write ( 'T' : w )
    ELSE
      write ( 'F' : w )
```

```
END; (* writebool *)
PROCEDURE showtable ( t   : boolarray;
                      rel : relation );

BEGIN
  CASE rel OF
    lt : write ('<');
    le : write ('<=');
    eq : write ('=');
    ge : write ('>=');
    gt : write ('>');
    ne : write ('<>')
  END; (* case *)
  write ('f': 4, 't': 4 );
  writeln;
  writeln ('********');
  write('f'); writebool ( t [ false, false ], 1 );
              writebool ( t [ false, true ], 4 );
  writeln;
  write ('t'); writebool ( t [ true , false ], 1 );
              writebool ( t [ true , true ], 4 );

  writeln
END; (* showtable *)

BEGIN (* truth *)
  FOR rel := lt TO ne DO
    BEGIN
      buildtable ( tt, rel );
      showtable ( tt, rel );
      writeln
    END (* for *)
END.
```

```
(* EXAMPLE PROGRAM 10 *)
PROGRAM printcalendars (output);
VAR  year : integer;

PROCEDURE calendar ( (* using *) y : integer );
CONST daynames = 'Sun  Mon Tues Wed Thurs Fri  Sat  ';
      m1 = ' January  '; m2 = ' February '; m3 = ' March    ';
      m4 = ' April    '; m5 = ' May      '; m6 = ' June     ';
      m7 = ' July     '; m8 = ' August   '; m9 = 'September ';
      m10= ' October  '; m11= ' November '; m12= ' December ';
      align  =  '                           '; align2 = '          -';
      errormessage = 'YEAR OUT OF RANGE';
      bottomline = 'Programmed in Pascal';
TYPE  month = ( jan, feb, mar, apr, may, jun,
                jul, aug, sep, oct, nov, dec );

      pseudoday = -5..43;
      monthname = PACKED ARRAY [1..10] OF char;
      dowtype = 0..6;
VAR   leap : boolean;
      dm  : ARRAY [month] OF pseudoday;
      dow : dowtype;
      m   : month;

FUNCTION divisible ( (* using *) a,b:integer)
                     (* returning *)          : boolean;

BEGIN
  divisible := a MOD b = 0
END; (* of divisible *)

PROCEDURE quarter ( (* using *)       s1,s2,s3 : monthname;
                    (* and *)         fm   : month;
                    (* updating *) VAR fdofm : dowtype );

VAR   row  : 1..6;
      i,sm,tm : month;
```

```pascal
         j      : 1..7;
         m      : ARRAY [month] OF pseudoday;
BEGIN (* quarter *)
   writeln; writeln; writeln; writeln;
   write ( s1:34 ); write ( s2:41 ); writeln ( s3:41 );
   writeln;
   sm := succ (fm);
   tm := succ (sm);
   write (align);        (* for alignment *)
   FOR i:= fm TO tm DO write (daynames);
   writeln; writeln;
   m[fm] := 1 - fdofm;
   m[fm] := 1 - ( 1 - m[fm] + dm[fm]) MOD 7;
   m[sm] := 1 - ( 1 - m[sm] + dm[sm]) MOD 7 ;
   fdofm := ( 1 - m[tm] + dm[tm]) MOD 7 ;
   FOR row := 1 TO 6 DO
   BEGIN (* row *)
      write(align2);
      FOR i := fm TO tm DO
      BEGIN (* one of three *)
         FOR j:= 1 TO 7 DO
         BEGIN (* day *)
            IF ( m[i] < 1 ) OR ( m[i] > dm [i] )
               THEN  write ('     ')

               ELSE  write ( m[i] : 5 );
            m[i]:= m[i] + 1
         END; (* day *)
         IF i <> tm THEN write ('          ');
      END; (* one of three *)
      writeln
```

Example Program 10 cont.

```
      END (* row *)
   END; (* quarter *)

BEGIN (* calendar *)
   IF y < 1753 THEN writeln (errormessage)
   ELSE
   BEGIN (* valid year *)
      dow := ((y - 1) + (y - 1) DIV 4 - (y - 1) DIV 100
              + (y - 1) DIV 400 + 1) MOD 7 ;

      leap := divisible(y,4) AND NOT divisible(y,100)
              OR divisible(y,400);

      FOR m := jan TO dec DO
         IF m IN [ apr, jun, sep, nov ]
            THEN dm[m] := 30

         ELSE
            dm[m] := 31;

      writeln ( y : 72 );
      IF leap

            THEN dm[feb] := 29
            ELSE dm[feb] := 28;

      quarter ( m1,m2,m3, jan, dow );
      quarter ( m4,m5,m6, apr, dow );
      quarter ( m7,m8,m9, jul, dow );
      quarter(m10,m11,m12,oct, dow );
      writeln; writeln;
      writeln ( bottomline )
   END; (* valid year *)
   page
END; (* calendar *)

BEGIN (* printcalendars *)
   calendar ( 1993 )
END. (* printcalendars *)
```

```
(* EXAMPLE PROGRAM 11 *)
PROGRAM anagram ( input, output );
(* generates the anagrams of a string of up to L characters
   BEWARE: There can be rather a lot!
           ( n factorial where n is length of string ) *)

CONST L = 10;           (* length of string *)
VAR  ln : PACKED ARRAY [ 1 .. L ] OF char;
     i : 1 .. L;
     len : 0 .. L;

PROCEDURE ReadLine;
CONST space = ' ';
VAR i : 1 .. L;
BEGIN
   len := 0;
   FOR i := 1 TO L DO
      IF eoln
         THEN
            ln [ i ] := space
         ELSE
            BEGIN
               read ( ln [ i ] );
               len := i
            END;
END; (* ReadLine *)

PROCEDURE juggle ( k : integer );
VAR i : 1 .. L;
   PROCEDURE SwapIK;
   VAR temp : char;
   BEGIN (* SwapIK *)
      temp := ln [ i ];
```

Example Program 11 cont.

```
            ln [ i ] := ln [ k];
            ln [ k ] := temp
   END; (* SwapIK *)
BEGIN (* juggle *)
   IF k = 1             (*terminating condition for recursion *)
      THEN
         writeln ( ln : len )
      ELSE
         BEGIN
            juggle ( k – 1 );      (*recursive call *)
            FOR i := 1 TO k – 1 DO
               BEGIN
                  SwapIK; (*interchange Ith and Kth elements of 1n *)
                  juggle ( k – 1 );     (* recursive call *)
                  Swap IK           (* change them back again *)
               END
         END

END (* juggle *)

BEGIN
   ReadLine;
   juggle ( len )
END (* anagram *)


(* EXAMPLE PROGRAM 12 *)
PROGRAM fogindex ( input, output );
(* Calculates 'fog index' of text
   given by :
```

```pascal
                0.4 x ( average-words-per-sentence + percentage-long )
                where long means three syllables or more.
                ( words of syll3 or more letters are taken to be 'long' *)

CONST wordlength = 20;           (* maximum length of a word *)
      syll3      = 10;           (* minimum length of word taken as 'long' *)
TYPE  kindtype  = ( word, stop, punct, endsym );
      index     = 1 .. wordlength;
      letters   = PACKED ARRAY [index] OF char;
      natural   = 0 .. maxint;
      symboltype = RECORD
                     CASE kind : kindtype OF
                       word  : ( contents : letters;
                                 length   : index );

                       stop,
                       punct,
                       endsym : ( (* empty *) )

                   END; (* case *)

VAR   symbol   : symboltype;
      words,
      extras,
      sentences,
      fog,
      longs    : natural;
      percentlongs,
      average  : real;
      lastwasstop,
      finish   : boolean;

FUNCTION alphabetic ( ch : char ) : boolean;
BEGIN
  (* a set [ 'A'..'Z', 'a'..'z' ] nicer if available *)
  alphabetic := ( ch >= 'A' ) AND ( ch <= 'I' ) OR
```

Example Program 12 cont.

```
                ( ch >= 'J' ) AND ( ch <= 'R' ) OR
                ( ch >= 'S' ) AND ( ch <= 'Z' ) OR
                ( ch >= 'a' ) AND ( ch <= 'i' ) OR
                ( ch >= 'j' ) AND ( ch <= 'r' ) OR
                ( ch >= 's' ) AND ( ch <= 'z' ) OR
END;
PROCEDURE readsymbol ( VAR symbol : symboltype );
CONST   space = ' ';
        period = '.';
        colon = ':';
VAR     L : index;
BEGIN
  WHILE NOT eof AND ( input^ = space ) DO
    get ( input );
  IF eof
    THEN
      symbol.kind := endsym
    ELSE WITH symbol DO
      BEGIN
        IF alphabetic ( input^ )
          THEN
            BEGIN
              kind := word;
              FOR L := 1 TO wordlength DO
                IF eof OR NOT alphabetic ( input^ )
                  THEN
                    contents [ L ] := space
                  ELSE
                    BEGIN
                      read ( contents [ L ] );
```

```
                    length := l
            END
      END (* alphabetic *)
    ELSE
      IF ( input^ = period ) OR ( input^ = colon )
      THEN
        BEGIN
          get ( input );
          IF ( input^ = space ) OR eof
          THEN
            BEGIN
              kind := stop;
              IF NOT eof
              THEN
                GET ( input )
            END
          ELSE
            kind := punct
        END

      ELSE
        BEGIN
          kind := punct;
          get ( input )
        END
  END; (* readsymbol *)
END (* with symbol *)
BEGIN (* fogindex *)
words := 0;
sentences := 0;
longs := 0;
extras := 0;
finish := false;
```

Example Program 12 cont.

```
lastwasstop := false;
REPEAT
   readsymbol ( symbol );
   WITH symbol DO
      CASE kind OF
         word  : BEGIN
                    lastwasstop := false;
                    words := words + 1;
                    IF length >= syll3
                       THEN
                          longs := longs + 1
                 END;
         stop  : BEGIN
                    lastwasstop := true;
                    sentences := sentences + 1
                 END;
         punct : BEGIN
                    lastwasstop := false;
                    extras := extras + 1
                 END;
         endsym: BEGIN
                    IF NOT lastwasstop
                       THEN
                          sentences := sentences + 1;
                    finish := true
                 END
      END  (* case *)
UNTIL finish;
IF words < 100
   THEN
      writeln ( 'Too few words - index will not be reliable');
```

```pascal
IF sentences > 0
  THEN
    BEGIN
      average := words / sentences;
      percentlongs := longs / words * 100.0;
      fog := round ( 0.4 * ( average + percentlongs ) );
      writeln('average words per sentence : ', average :
              10 : 3 );
      writeln( ' number of words : ', words : 5 );
      writeln( 'number of sentences : ', sentences : 3 );
      writeln( 'words of 3 or more syllables : ',
               percentlongs : 7 : 2, '%');
      writeln;
      writeln(' F o g  I n d e x  :  ', fog : 3 )
    END
  ELSE
    writeln ('NO CHARACTERS ON INPUT FILE ')
END. (* fogindex *)

(* EXAMPLE PROGRAM 13 *)
PROGRAM down ( input, output );
(* Shifts from upper case to lower *)

VAR ch, newch : char;
BEGIN
  WHILE NOT eof DO
    BEGIN
      WHILE NOT eoln DO
        BEGIN
          read ( ch );
          (* Assumes continuous alphabetics
             IF ch IN [ 'a' .. 'z' ]
             better if SETS OF char available *)
          IF ( ch >= 'A' ) AND ( ch <= 'Z' )
```

Example Program 13 cont.

```
                THEN
                    newch := chr ( ord ( ch ) + ord ( 'a' ) - ord ( 'A' ) )
                ELSE
                    newch := ch;
                write ( newch )
            END; (* WHILE NOT eoln *)
        writeln;
        readln
    END (* WHILE NOT eof *)
END. (* down *)


(* EXAMPLE PROGRAM 14 *)
PROGRAM alfa (input,output);
(* Counts frequencies of alphabetic characters in text *)

TYPE cardinal   = 0 .. maxint;
VAR  ch, capch  : char;
     counter    : ARRAY [ char ] OF cardinal;
     total      : cardinal;

FUNCTION cap ( ch : char ) : char;
BEGIN
    IF ch IN [ 'a' .. 'z' ]
        THEN
            cap := chr (ord ('A') + ord (ch) - ord ('a') )
        ELSE
            cap := ch
END; (* cap *)
    BEGIN
```

```
FOR ch := 'A' TO 'Z' DO
    counter [ ch ] := 0;
total := 0;
WHILE NOT eof DO
    BEGIN
    read ( ch );
    total := total + 1;
    capch := cap ( ch );
    IF capch IN [ 'A' .. 'Z']
        THEN
            counter [ capch ] := counter [ capch ] + 1
    END;
writeln ('   Character ' : 10 , 'Frequency' : 10,
                                 'Percentage' : 20 );
FOR ch := 'a' TO 'z' DO
    writeln ( ' ', ch : 10, counter [ ch ] : 10 ,
                            counter [ ch ] / total * 100 : 20 : 3 )

END. (* alfa *)


(* EXAMPLE PROGRAM 15 *)
PROGRAM Soundex ( input, output );
(* Program to convert names to the 'Soundex' system.
( Used to avoid difficulties due to misspelling ).
Take first letter of name then encode remaining letters as follows:
    BCD FG   JKLMN PQRST V X Z
    123 12   22455 12623 1 2 2
    Vowels and 'W', 'H' and 'Y' are ignored.
Use only first three digits, fill with zeros at right if necessary.
Examples: Pascal   becomes P224
```

Example Program 15 cont.

```
          Modula-2  becomes  M340
          Ada       becomes  A300
          Byrne     becomes  B650
          Burn      becomes  B650  *)

CONST  maxline = 25;           (* maximum length of names to be considered *)
       space   = ' ';
       term    = '*';          (* terminator character for keyboard *)

VAR    line   : PACKED ARRAY [ 1 .. maxline ] OF char;
       encode : PACKED ARRAY [ 'A' .. 'Z' ] OF 1 .. 6;
       i      : 1 .. maxline;
       j, k   : 0 .. 3;
       ch     : char;

FUNCTION cap ( ch : char ) : char;
(* gives upper-case equivalent of a character *)
BEGIN
  IF ch IN [ 'a' .. 'z' ]
  THEN
    CASE ch OF
      'a' : cap := 'A';   'b' : cap := 'B';   'c' : cap := 'C';
      'd' : cap := 'D';   'e' : cap := 'E';   'f' : cap := 'F';
      'g' : cap := 'G';   'h' : cap := 'H';   'i' : cap := 'I';
      'j' : cap := 'J';   'k' : cap := 'K';   'l' : cap := 'L';
      'm' : cap := 'M';   'n' : cap := 'N';   'o' : cap := 'O';
      'p' : cap := 'P';   'q' : cap := 'Q';   'r' : cap := 'R';
      's' : cap := 'S';   't' : cap := 'T';   'u' : cap := 'U';
      'v' : cap := 'V';   'w' : cap := 'W';   'x' : cap := 'X';
      'y' : cap := 'Y';   'z' : cap := 'Z'
    END (* case *)
  ELSE
    cap := ch
```

```
END; (* cap *)
BEGIN (* Soundex *)
  (* set up table for codings *)
  encode [ 'B' ] := 1;   encode [ 'C' ] := 2;   encode [ 'D' ] := 3;
  encode [ 'F' ] := 1;   encode [ 'G' ] := 2;   encode [ 'J' ] := 2;
  encode [ 'K' ] := 2;   encode [ 'L' ] := 4;   encode [ 'M' ] := 5;
  encode [ 'N' ] := 5;   encode [ 'P' ] := 1;   encode [ 'Q' ] := 2;
  encode [ 'R' ] := 6;   encode [ 'S' ] := 2;   encode [ 'T' ] := 3;
  encode [ 'V' ] := 1;   encode [ 'X' ] := 2;   encode [ 'Z' ] := 2;
WHILE NOT eof AND ( input^ <> term ) DO
  BEGIN
    (* skip characters that are not alphabetical *)
    WHILE NOT eoln AND NOT ( cap ( input^ ) IN [ 'A' .. 'Z' ] ) DO
      get ( input );
    (* read name *)
    FOR i := 1 TO maxline DO
      IF eoln
        THEN
          line [ i ] := space
        ELSE
          read ( line [ i ] );
    write ( line );
    (* form Soundex equivalent *)
    write ( cap ( line [ 1 ] ) : 5 );
    k := 0;
    FOR i := 2 TO maxline DO
      BEGIN
        ch := cap ( line [ i ] );
        IF ( ch IN ['B'..'D', 'F', 'G', 'J'..'N', 'P', 'T',
                    'V','X','Z' ] )
          AND ( k < 3 )
          THEN
```

Example Program 15 cont.

```
            BEGIN
              k := k + 1;
              write ( encode [ ch ] : 1 )
            END
      END; (* for *)
      FOR j := k TO 2 DO
        write ( '0' : 1 );
      writeln;
      readln
    END (* while *)
END. (* Soundex *)


(* EXAMPLE PROGRAM 16 *)
PROGRAM ReservedWordsInCaps ( input, output );
{ Text formatter to put Pascal reserved words into upper case and to put
  other identifiers into lower case, ignoring comments and strings }
CONST IdLength    = 32;    { maximum length of identifiers }
      quote       = '''';
      space       = ' ';
      NumRes      = 35;     { number of reserved words }
TYPE  WordString = PACKED ARRAY [ 1 .. IdLength ] OF char;
VAR   id        : WordString;
      ch        : char;
      i, j      : 0 .. MaxInt;
      WordTable : ARRAY [ 1 .. NumRes ] OF WordString;

FUNCTION CAP ( ch : char ) : char;
BEGIN
  IF ch IN [ 'a' .. 'z' ]
```

```
        THEN
          CAP := chr ( ord ( ch ) + ord ('A') - ord ('a') )
        ELSE
          CAP := ch
END; { CAP }

FUNCTION low ( ch : char ) : char;
BEGIN
  IF ch IN [ 'A' .. 'Z' ]
    THEN
      low := chr ( ord ( ch ) + ord ('a') - ord ('A') )
    ELSE
      low := ch
END; { low }

FUNCTION ReservedWord : Boolean;
VAR left , right , middle : 0 .. MaxInt;
BEGIN
  { binary search in table for reserved word }
  left := 1;
  right := NumRes;
  REPEAT
    middle := ( left + right ) DIV 2;
    IF id <= WordTable [ middle ]
      THEN
        right := middle - 1;
    IF id >= WordTable [ middle ]
      THEN
        left := middle + 1
  UNTIL left > right;
  ReservedWord := left - 1 <> right
END; { ReservedWord }
PROCEDURE copy;
```

Example Program 16 cont.

```
BEGIN
  IF eoln
  THEN
      BEGIN
        writeln;
        readln
      END
  ELSE
      BEGIN
        read ( ch );
        write ( ch )
      END
END; { copy }
BEGIN { ReservedWordsInCaps }
  WordTable [ 1 ] := 'AND
  WordTable [ 2 ] := 'ARRAY
  WordTable [ 3 ] := 'BEGIN
  WordTable [ 4 ] := 'CASE
  WordTable [ 5 ] := 'CONST
  WordTable [ 6 ] := 'DIV
  WordTable [ 7 ] := 'DO
  WordTable [ 8 ] := 'DOWNTO
  WordTable [ 9 ] := 'ELSE
  WordTable [ 10 ] := 'END
  WordTable [ 11 ] := 'FILE
  WordTable [ 12 ] := 'FOR
  WordTable [ 13 ] := 'FUNCTION
  WordTable [ 14 ] := 'GOTO
  WordTable [ 15 ] := 'IF
  WordTable [ 16 ] := 'IN
  WordTable [ 17 ] := 'LABEL
```

```
WordTable [ 18 ] := 'MOD       ';
WordTable [ 19 ] := 'NIL       ';
WordTable [ 20 ] := 'NOT       ';
WordTable [ 21 ] := 'OF        ';
WordTable [ 22 ] := 'OR        ';
WordTable [ 23 ] := 'PACKED    ';
WordTable [ 24 ] := 'PROCEDURE ';
WordTable [ 25 ] := 'PROGRAM   ';
WordTable [ 26 ] := 'RECORD    ';
WordTable [ 27 ] := 'REPEAT    ';
WordTable [ 28 ] := 'SET       ';
WordTable [ 29 ] := 'THEN      ';
WordTable [ 30 ] := 'TO        ';
WordTable [ 31 ] := 'TYPE      ';
WordTable [ 32 ] := 'UNTIL     ';
WordTable [ 33 ] := 'VAR       ';
WordTable [ 34 ] := 'WHILE     ';
WordTable [ 35 ] := 'WITH      ';
WHILE NOT eof DO
  BEGIN
    IF input^ IN [ 'A' .. 'Z', 'a' .. 'z' ]
      THEN
      BEGIN { identifier }
        i := 0;
        REPEAT
          read ( ch );
          i := i + 1;
          id [ i ] := CAP ( ch )
        UNTIL NOT(input^ IN['A' .. 'Z','a' .. 'z','0' .. '9']);
        FOR j := i + 1 TO IdLength DO
          id [ j ] := space;

        IF ReservedWord
```

Example Program 16 cont.

```
        THEN
            FOR j := 1 TO i DO
                write ( CAP ( id [ j ] ) )
        ELSE
            FOR j := 1 TO i DO
                write ( low ( id [ j ] ) );
END { identifier }
IF input^ = quote
    THEN
        BEGIN { character string }
            REPEAT
                copy
            UNTIL input^ = quote;
            copy { character string }
        END { character string }
    ELSE
IF input^ = '{'
    THEN
        BEGIN { comment }
            REPEAT
                copy;
            UNTIL input^ = '}';
            copy { comment }
        END { comment }
    ELSE
IF input^ = '('
    THEN
        BEGIN
            copy;
            IF input^ = '*'
```

```
                THEN
                    BEGIN (* comment *)
                        REPEAT
                            REPEAT
                                copy
                            UNTIL input^ = '*';
                            copy
                        UNTIL input^ = ')';
                        copy  (* comment *)
                    END
                ELSE
            END
                copy { some other character }
    END { WHILE NOT eof }
END. { ReservedWordsInCaps }


(* EXAMPLE PROGRAM 17 *)
PROGRAM Exam ( (* reading from *)  CandFile,
               (* writing to   *)  output );

(* This is a program to score examinations for a college. Students in
Business Studies take five subjects : Computer Science, Statistics,
English, Law and Economics. To pass the student must score more than the
PassMark in Statistics and on the average of all five subjects.
    In addition, the student must not fail more than two exams.
Students who achieve an average score above a certain mark ( and who have
passed ) will be awarded a Credit. Those who score above another ( higher )
mark will be awarded a Distinction. *)

CONST NameLength = 20;        (* length of character string holding student's
                                                                    name *)
```

Example Program 17 cont.

```
        MaxOnPage = 5;           (* number of student results per page *)
        NumSubjs  = 5;           (* number of subjects taken in examination *)
        FailLimit = 2;           (* number of subjects student is permitted to
                                                                      fail *)

        PassMark   = 40;         (* levels for each grade *)
        CreditMark = 60;
        DistMark   = 70;
TYPE    PosInt = 0 .. MaxInt;    (* type definition for positive integer
                                                                       *)

        SubjType  = ( CompSci, statistics, english, law, economics );
        GradeType = ( fail, pass, credit, distinction );
        FailSet   = SET OF SubjType;
        PassArray = ARRAY [ SubjType ] OF PosInt;
        CandType  = RECORD
                      CandNo   : PACKED ARRAY [ 1 .. 5 ] OF char;
                      CandName : PACKED ARRAY [ 1 .. NameLength ] OF char;
                      marks    : ARRAY [ SubjType ] OF 0 .. 100
                    END; (* record *)

VAR     FileOfCand = FILE OF CandType;
        CandRec    : CandType;
        CandFile   : FileOfCand;
        PageNumber,              (* used by procedure "headings" *)
        NumOnPage,               (* used by procedure "CheckPage" *)
        TotalCands,
        TotalPasses: PosInt;
        SubjPasses : PassArray;
        average    : real;
        WhatFailed : FailSet;
        grade      : GradeType;
PROCEDURE initialise ( (* returning *) VAR TotalPasses,
                                           PageNumber,
```

```
                                  NumOnPage,
                                  TotalCands    : PosInt;
                              VAR SubjPasses    : PassArray;
                              VAR CandFile      : FileOfCand );

(* sets initial values *)
VAR  sub : SubjType;
BEGIN
     reset ( CandFile );        (* load buffer with first record *)
     TotalPasses := 0;
     TotalCands := 0;
     PageNumber := 0;
     NumOnPage :=0;
     FOR sub := CompSci TO economics DO
          SubjPasses [ sub ] := 0
END; (* initialise *)

PROCEDURE ReadCand (    (* returning *) VAR CandRec : CandType;
                        (* using *)     VAR CandFile : FileOfCand );

(* reads next record from CandFile *)
BEGIN
     CandRec := CandFile^;      (* gets record from buffer *)
     get ( CandFile )           (* refills buffer           *)
END; (* ReadCand *)

PROCEDURE AnalyseMark (  (* using *)     VAR CandRec  : CandType;
                         (* returning *) VAR grade    : GradeType;
                                         VAR average  : real;
                                         VAR WhatFailed : FailSet );

(* discovers average mark and grade for current student *)
VAR  NumFails : 0 .. NumSubjs;
     TotalMark : PosInt;
     sub : SubjType;
     ThisMark : 0 .. 100;
     failed : Boolean;
```

Example Program 17 cont.

```
BEGIN
  NumFails := 0;
  TotalMark := 0;
  WhatFailed := [ ];    (* the empty set *)
  WITH CandRec DO
    BEGIN
    FOR sub := CompSci TO economics DO
      BEGIN
      ThisMark := marks [ sub ];
      TotalMark := TotalMark + ThisMark;
      IF ThisMark < PassMark
        THEN
          BEGIN
          WhatFailed := WhatFailed + [ sub ];
          NumFails := NumFails + 1
          END (* IF *)
      END (* FOR *)
    END; (* WITH *)
  average := TotalMark / NumSubjs;
  failed := ( statistics IN WhatFailed ) OR
            ( NumFails > FailLimit ) OR
            ( average < PassMark );
  IF failed
    THEN
      grade := fail
    ELSE IF average < CreditMark
      THEN
        grade := pass
      ELSE
        If average < DistMark
```

```
          THEN
               grade := credit
          ELSE grade := distinction
END; (* AnalyseMarks *)

PROCEDURE UpdateTotals (   (* using    *)       grade        : GradeType;
                                                WhatFailed   : FailSet;
                           (* returning *) VAR SubjPasses : PassArray;
                                           VAR TotalPasses,
                                               TotalCands : PosInt );

(* updates counters of passes *)
VAR  sub : SubjType;
BEGIN
   TotalCands := TotalCands + 1;
   IF grade >= pass
   THEN
      TotalPasses := TotalPasses + 1;
   FOR sub := CompSci TO economics DO
      IF NOT ( sub IN WhatFailed )
      THEN
         SubjPasses [ sub ] := SubjPasses [ sub ] + 1
END; (* UpdateTotals *)

PROCEDURE headings (  (* updating *) PageNumber : PosInt );
(* print headings for output report *)
CONST title   = 'Business Studies Final Examination';
      college = 'ACME College of Management and Commerce';

BEGIN
   PageNumber := PageNumber + 1;
   page ( output );
   writeln( college, '     ', title, '     ', 'page ', PageNumber : 4 );
   writeln;
```

Example Program 17 cont.

```
            writeln
      END; (* headings *)

      PROCEDURE CheckPage (     (* updating *) VAR NumOnPage,
                                (* passing *)      PageNumber : PosInt );

      (* tests whether page throw required *)
      BEGIN
        NumOnPage := NumOnPage + 1;
        IF NumOnPage > MaxOnPage
          THEN
            BEGIN
              headings ( (* updating *) PageNumber );
              NumOnPage := 0
            END
      END; (* CheckPage *)

      PROCEDURE WriteResult (    (* using *)  CandRec    : CandType;
                                              grade      : GradeType;
                                              WhatFailed : FailSet;
                                              average    : real );

      (* writes out the results for current student *)
      VAR  sub : SubjType;
      BEGIN
        WITH CandRec DO
          BEGIN
            writeln ( CandNo, '   ', CandName );
            writeln;
            FOR sub := CompSci TO economics DO
              BEGIN
                write ('            ');
                CASE sub OF
                  CompSci    : write ('Computer science ');
```

```pascal
                statistics : write ('Statistics          ');
                english    : write ('English             ');
                law        : write ('Law                 ');
                economics  : write ('Economics           ')
              END; (* CASE *)
              write ( marks [ sub ] : 4 );
              IF sub IN WhatFailed
              THEN
                write ( '  *** FAIL *** ' );
            END
          END (* FOR *)
        END (* WITH *)
        writeln
        write ('          average mark ', average : 6 : 2 );
        write ('          overall grade ');
        CASE grade OF
          fail        : write ('*** FAILED *** ');
          pass        : write ('PASS');
          credit      : write ('CREDIT');
          distinction : write ('DISTINCTION')
        END; (* CASE *)
        writeln
      END; (* WriteResult *)

PROCEDURE WriteTotals ( (* using *) SubjPasses  : PassArray;
                                    TotalPasses,
                                    TotalCands  : PosInt );
(* writes out total passes and percentages *)
CONST left  = ' Comp. Science Statistics English     ';
      right = 'Law Economics Overall';
VAR   factor : real;
      sub : SubjType;
```

Example Program 17 cont.

```
BEGIN
   factor := 100.0 / TotalCands;
   writeln;
   writeln ( left, right );
   write ('Totals        ');
   FOR sub := CompSci TO economics DO
      write ( SubjPasses [ sub ] : 12 );

   writeln;
   write ( 'Percentage ' );
   FOR sub := CompSci TO economics DO
      write ( SubjPasses [ sub ] * factor : 12 : 2 );
   writeln
END; (* WriteTotals *)

PROCEDURE RoomForTotals (    (* using *)    NumOnPage : PosInt;
                             (* passing *) VAR PageNumber : PosInt );

(* makes sure there is room on page for totals *)
BEGIN
   IF NumOnPage >= MaxOnPage
   THEN
      headings ( (* updating *) PageNumber )

END; (* RoomForTotals *)

BEGIN (* Exam *)
   initialise ( (* updating *) Totalpasses,
                               PageNumber,
                               NumOnPage,
                               TotalCands,
                               SubjPasses,
                               CandFile );

   headings ( (* updating *) PageNumber );
   WHILE NOT eof ( CandFile ) DO
```

```
BEGIN
    ReadCand      (  (* obtaining *)  CandRec,
                     (* from *)       Candfile );
    AnalyseMark   (  (* using *)      CandRec,
                     (* obtaining *)  grade,
                                      average,
                                      WhatFailed );
    CheckPage     (  (* updating *)   NumOnPage,
                                      PageNumber );
    WriteResult   (  (* using *)      CandRec,
                                      grade,
                                      WhatFailed,
                                      average );
    UpdateTotals  (  (* using *)      grade,
                                      WhatFailed,
                                      SubjPasses,
                                      TotalPasses,
                                      TotalCands )
    END; (* while *)
    RoomForTotals (  (* using *)      NumOnPage,
                                      PageNumber );
    WriteTotals   (  (* using *)      SubjPasses,
                                      TotalPasses,
                                      TotalCands )
END. (* Exam *)
```

```
(* EXAMPLE PROGRAM 18 *)
PROGRAM treesort ( input, output );
(* Sorts by building tree and traversing in appropriate order
   uses recursive procedures and pointers *)
TYPE valtype = real;    (* can be any type for which comparisons can be made *)

     ptr    = ^ node;
     node   = RECORD
                    left  : ptr;
                    val   : valtype;
                    right : ptr
              END; (* node *)

VAR  tree  : ptr;
     inval : valtype;

PROCEDURE buildtree ( (* inserting *)  x : valtype;
                      (* in *) VAR  t : ptr );
(* builds tree by placing new node at end of appropriate branch *)
BEGIN
  IF t = NIL
  THEN
     BEGIN                          (* put in new node *)
        new ( t );
        WITH t^ DO
           BEGIN
              left  := NIL;
              val   := x;
              right := NIL
           END; (* with *)
     END
  ELSE
     IF x < t^.val
```

```
                THEN
                    buildtree ( x, t^.left  )
                ELSE
                    buildtree ( x, t^.right )
END; (* buildtree *)


PROCEDURE traverse ( VAR t : ptr );
(* traverses tree - go left, write value, go right - recursively *)
BEGIN
    IF t <> NIL
        THEN
            BEGIN
                traverse ( t^.left );
                writeln ( t^.val );
                traverse ( t^.right)
            END
END; (* traverse *)


BEGIN (* treesort - main program *)
    tree := nil;
    WHILE NOT eof DO
        BEGIN
            readln ( inval );
            buildtree ( (* inserting *) inval,
                        (* in *)        tree )
        END; (* while *)
    traverse ( tree )
END. (* treesort *)
```

Index

COMPUTER PROGRAMMING IN BASIC

L. R. CARTER and E. HUZAN

BASIC (Beginners All-purpose Symbolic Instruction Code) is a widely used programming language in education, commerce and industry, particularly for mini- and microcomputers, and by the hobbyist.

A knowledge of BASIC provides a useful introduction to computer programming and allows effective practical applications to be developed on many systems.

This book provides a practical grounding in BASIC. An elementary description of the functions of a computer is followed by an explanation of the purpose of system commands for running BASIC programs. There are also chapters on program development and testing. Exercises are provided throughout and answers to problems and suggested programs are given in appendices. The final chapter of the book illustrates the use of BASIC for a range of simple mathematical, scientific and business applications.

TEACH YOURSELF BOOKS

COMPUTER PROGRAMMING IN COBOL

MELINDA FISHER

COBOL (COmmon Business Oriented Language) is the computer language which is most widely used in business and commerce, for invoicing, stock control, payroll and management information systems, on both microcomputer and mainframe installations.

This book looks first at the basic concepts of computers and computer programming before examining the language, logic design and special features of COBOL. Starting from first principles, the book systematically introduces and explains the main COBOL facilities, language statements and relevant syntax. Thus the reader progresses in easy stages from data description and manipulation, through sequence control and handling sequential files and tables, to producing printed reports and indexing. Sample programs illustrate the everyday application of COBOL facilities and a fully documented example shows how a tested, working program is developed from an initial specification. Exercises (with answers) are provided throughout.

TEACH YOURSELF BOOKS

COMPUTER PROGRAMMING IN FORTRAN

ARTHUR S. RADFORD

FORTRAN (FORmula TRANslator) is an established computer language, which has been widely adopted for scientific, technical and commercial applications.

This book provides a step-by-step introduction to FORTRAN 77 – the most up-to-date standard version of the language. Arthur Radford looks first at the basic concepts of computing and program design before explaining the syntax and structure of FORTRAN. He then describes the system commands for programming conditional statements, loops, arrays and subroutines, and the input and output requirements, including file processing. A wide range of illustrative examples and exercises (with answers) gives the beginner a practical grounding in FORTRAN programming while a comparison with the earlier standard FORTRAN 66 makes the book suitable also as a conversion course for more experienced programmers.

TEACH YOURSELF BOOKS